On Rumors

Also by Cass R. Sunstein

On Rumors

How Falsehoods Spread,
Why We Believe Them,
and What Can Be Done

Cass R. Sunstein

With a new afterword by the author

Princeton University Press · Princeton and Oxford

Requests for permission to reproduce material from this work should be sent to
    Permissions, Princeton University Press
Published by Princeton University Press, 41 William Street, Princeton, New Jersey
    08540
In the United Kingdom: Princeton University Press, 6 Oxford Street, Woodstock,
    Oxfordshire OX20 1TW
press.princeton.edu

Originally published in North America by Farrar, Straus and Giroux in 2009

First Princeton Edition 2014

ISBN (pbk.) 978-0-691-16250-8

LCCN 2013950544

British Library Cataloging-in-Publication Data is available

This book has been composed in Adobe Caslon

Printed on acid-free paper. ∞

Printed in the United States of America

10 9 8 7 6 5 4 3 2 1

For Declan

Each rumor has its own public.

—Gordon Allport and Leo Postman, *The Psychology of Rumor*

Contents

On Rumors

The Problem

Rumors are nearly as old as human history, but with the rise of the Internet, they have become ubiquitous. In fact we are now awash in them. False rumors are especially troublesome; they impose real damage on individuals and institutions, and they often resist correction. They can threaten careers, relationships, policies, public officials, democracy, and sometimes even peace itself.

Many of the most pervasive rumors involve governments—what officials are planning and why. Others involve famous people in politics, business, and entertainment, or companies, large and small. Still others involve people who are not at all in the public eye. On Facebook and on

1

Twitter, everyone is at some risk. All of us are potentially victims of rumors, including false and vicious ones.

In recent years, many Americans have believed that Barack Obama was a Muslim, that he was not born in the United States, and that he "pals around with terrorists." Rumors are pervasive about the allegedly terrible acts, beliefs, and motivations of public officials and about the allegedly scandalous private lives not only of those officials, but also of many other people with a high public profile. Rumors can harm the economy as well. If it is rumored that a company is about to fail, stockholders may well be frightened, and they might sell. Because of the rumor, the company might fail. Rumors can and do affect the stock market itself, even if they are baseless. It should not be entirely surprising that the Securities and Exchange Commission has taken a keen interest in the pernicious effects of false rumors, and that New York has made it a crime to circulate false rumors about the financial status of banks. Rumors can increase international tensions and perhaps produce sparks that culminate in violence.

2 In the era of the Internet, it has become easy to spread false or misleading rumors about almost anyone. A high school student, a salesperson, a professor, a banker, an employer, an insurance broker, a real estate agent—each of these is vulnerable to an allegation that can have a painful, damaging, or even devastating effect. If an allegation of misconduct appears on the Internet, those who Google the relevant name will immediately learn about it. The allegation will help to define the person. (It might even end up on Wikipedia, at least for a time.) The rumor can involve organizations as well as individuals—the Central Intelligence

Agency, General Motors, Bank of America, the Boy Scouts, the Catholic Church. Material on the Internet has considerable longevity. For all practical purposes, it may be permanent. For this reason, a false rumor can have an enduring effect.

This small book has two goals. The first is to answer these questions: Why do ordinary human beings accept rumors, even false, destructive, and bizarre ones? Why do some groups, and even nations, accept rumors that other groups and nations deem preposterous? The second is to answer this question: What can we do to protect ourselves against the harmful effects of false rumors? As we shall see, part of the answer lies in recognizing that a "chilling effect" on those who would spread destructive falsehoods can be a truly excellent idea, especially if those falsehoods amount to libel.

We will also see that when people believe rumors, they are often perfectly rational, in the sense that their belief is quite sensible in light of their existing knowledge—of what they now know. We lack direct or personal knowledge about the facts that underlie most of our judgments. How do you know that the earth isn't flat? That Shakespeare really existed? That matter is made of atoms? That the Holocaust actually occurred? That Lee Harvey Oswald assassinated President Kennedy? Most of our knowledge is at best indirect about other people, other nations, other cultures, other religions. We rarely know for sure whether a particular company is in terrible trouble or whether a particular public official has taken a bribe, or whether an influential person has a secret agenda or a shameful incident in her past. Lacking personal knowledge, we tend to think that where there is smoke, there is fire—or that a rumor would not have spread unless it was at least partly true. Perhaps the truth is even worse than the rumor. Certainly we should be cautious before entrusting our nation or our company to the hands of someone who is rumored to have said or done bad things. Our willingness to think in this way causes special problems when we rely on the Internet for our information, simply because false rumors are so pervasive there.

There is no settled definition of rumors, and I will not attempt to offer one here. To get the discussion off the ground, let us acknowledge the crudeness of any definition, put semantic debates to one side, and take the term to refer roughly to claims of fact—about people, groups, events, and institutions—that have not been shown to be true, but that move from one person to another, and hence have credibility not because direct evidence is available to support them, but because other people seem to believe them. So understood, rumors often arise and gain traction because they fit with, and support, the prior convictions of those who accept them. Some people and some groups are predisposed to accept certain rumors because those rumors are compatible with their self-interest, or with what they think they know to be true. Some people are strongly motivated to accept certain rumors, because it pleases them to do so. In 2008, many Americans were prepared to believe that Governor Sarah Palin thought that Africa was a country rather than a continent, because that ridiculous mistake fit with what they already thought about Governor Palin. Other people were predisposed to reject the same rumor. Exposure to the same information spurred radically different beliefs.

Many of us accept false rumors because of either our fears or our hopes. Because we fear al-Qaeda, we are more inclined to believe that its members are plotting an attack near where we live. Because we hope that our favorite company will prosper, we might believe a rumor that its new product cannot fail and that its prospects are about to soar. In the context of war, one group's fears are unmistakably another group's hopes—and whenever groups compete, the fears of some are the hopes of others. Because rumors fuel some fears and alleviate others, radically different reactions to the same rumor are inevitable. The citizens of Iran or Iraq or China may accept a rumor that has no traction in Canada or France or Ireland. Those in Utah may accept a rumor that seems preposterous in Massachusetts. Republicans accept rumors that Democrats ridicule, and vice versa. And to the extent that the Internet enables people to live in information cocoons, or echo chambers of their own design, different rumors will become entrenched in different communities.

Many rumors spread conspiracy theories.[1] Consider the rumor that the Central Intelligence Agency was responsible for the assassination of President John F. Kennedy; that doctors deliberately manufactured the AIDS virus; that the idea of climate change is a deliberate fraud; that Martin Luther King, Jr., was killed by federal agents; that the plane crash that killed Democratic senator Paul Wellstone was engineered by Republican politicians; that the moon landing was staged; that the Rothschilds and other Jewish bankers are responsible for the deaths of presidents and for economic distress in Asian nations; and that the Great Depression was a result of a plot by wealthy people to reduce the wages of workers.[2] Or consider the work of the French author Thierry Meyssan, whose book *9/11: The Big Lie* became a best seller and a sensation for its claims that the Pentagon explosion on 9/11 was caused by a missile, fired as the opening salvo of a coup d'état by the military-industrial complex, rather than by American Airlines Flight 77.[3]

Rumors spread through two different but overlapping processes: *social cascades* and *group polarization*. Cascades occur because each of us tends to rely on what other people think and do. If most of the people we know believe a rumor, we tend to believe it too. Lacking information of our own, we accept the views of others. When the rumor involves a topic on which we know nothing, we are especially likely to believe it. If the National Rifle Association spreads a rumor that a political candidate wants to "confiscate guns," or if an environmental organization spreads a rumor that someone believes that climate change is "a hoax," many people will be affected, because they tend to believe the National Rifle Association or the environmental organization.

A cascade occurs when a group of early movers say or do something and other people follow their signal. In the economy, rumors can fuel speculative bubbles, greatly inflating prices, and indeed speculative bubbles help to account for the financial crisis of 2008. Rumors are also responsible for many panics, as fear spreads rapidly from one person to another, creating self-fulfilling prophecies. And if the relevant rumors trigger strong emotions, such as fear or disgust, they are far more likely to spread.

Group polarization refers to the fact that when like-minded people get together, they often end up thinking a more extreme version of what they thought before they started to talk to one another.[4] Suppose that members of a certain group are inclined to accept a rumor about, say, the malevolent intentions of an apparently unfriendly group or nation. In all likelihood, they will become more committed to that rumor after they have spoken among themselves. Indeed, they may have moved from being tentative believers to being absolutely certain that the rumor is true, even though all they know is what other group members think. Consider the role of the Internet here: any one of us might receive numerous communications from many of us, and when we receive those communications, we might think that whatever is being said is probably true, especially if we hear it from lots of people. Volume can speak volumes.

What can be done to reduce the risk that cascades and polarization will lead people to accept false rumors? The most obvious answer, and the standard one, involves the system of free expression: people should be exposed to balanced information and to corrections from those who know the truth. That standard answer remains mostly right, and its importance cannot be overstated. Fortunately, freedom usually works. Unfortunately, it can be an incomplete corrective. Emotions can get in the way of truth seeking. People do not process information in a neutral way. Their preconceptions affect their reactions. *Biased assimilation* refers to the fact that people process new information in a biased fashion; those who have accepted false rumors may not easily give up their beliefs, especially when they have a strong emotional commitment to those beliefs. It can be exceedingly hard to dislodge what people think, even by presenting them with the facts. That presentation might cause them to become more entrenched.

Many people enthusiastically believe in the "marketplace of ideas." They think that the marketplace is the best way to ensure that people arrive at the truth. In one of the greatest opinions in all of American law, Justice Oliver Wendell Holmes argued that "the ultimate good desired is better reached by free trade in ideas—that the best test of truth is the power of the thought to get itself accepted in the competition of the market."[5] This powerful claim has exerted an enduring and salutary influence on the law of free speech, not merely in the United States but throughout the world. It continues to capture a commitment that all free societies accept.

For some rumors, however, the marketplace works exceedingly poorly, and it can be the problem, not the solution. Consider, for example, the potential consequences of a rumor of criminal behavior by a neighbor of yours, someone with no access to the media and without credibility on the Internet. Or suppose that an emotionally gripping rumor is starting to spread about the leader of a local company or a high-level political official. Far from being the best test of truth, the marketplace can ensure that many people accept falsehoods, or that they take mere fragments of lives, or small events, as representative of some alarming whole. The problem is serious and pervasive and—with the growing influence of the Internet and new kinds of surveillance—it seems to be increasing. On occasion, it results in serious harm to people's lives, damages the prospects of businesses, hurts investors, and undermines democracy itself.

We should underline the last point in particular. Free speech is meant, in part, to promote self-government; a well-functioning democracy cannot exist unless people are able to say what they think, even if what they think is false. But if people spread false rumors—most obviously about public officials and institutions—democracy itself will suffer. For no good reason, people might lose faith in particular leaders and policies, and even in their government itself. At the same time, false rumors impede our ability to think well, as citizens, about those who do or might lead, or about what to do about a crisis, whether large or small.

These points should not be taken as a plea for any kind of censorship. It is true and important that any effort to regulate speech will create a "chilling effect." Punish people for spreading falsehoods, and you will find yourself "chilling" truth. Suppose that the law will hold people accountable if they circulate a false rumor about a bank. To be sure, it is good if people are not injured as a result of that false rumor. But that very law might discourage someone else from disclosing, on the basis of credible evidence, the fact that a bank is in real trouble. Pointing to the risk of a chilling effect on free speech and hence on the transmission of truth, reasonable people often suggest that the government should allow a great deal of breathing space for falsehoods, even damaging ones. They suggest that the less regulation of the marketplace, the better.

Under reasonable assumptions, they are probably right. But there is a countervailing consideration. Sometimes a chilling effect can be an excellent safeguard. Without such an effect, the marketplace of ideas will lead many people to spread and to accept damaging falsehoods about both individuals and institutions. If false rumors create serious problems, we have to be careful to ensure that the fear of a chilling effect does not itself have a chilling effect on public discussion or on our practices. These falsehoods can hurt or even ruin individual lives. They can also have serious economic consequences. This risk is precisely what led New York to enact a law making it a crime to spread false rumors about banks. As we have seen, false rumors can undermine democracy itself. For all these reasons, it is sensible to hope that social norms and even law will impose a certain chill on them. We need, in short, to find ways to discourage belief in false and damaging rumors.

One of my major goals here is to sketch the mechanisms that lie behind false rumors—their propagation, their transmission, and their entrenchment. Many of those who seek to spread rumors have an intuitive awareness of those mechanisms; sometimes their understanding is highly sophisticated. Many propagators know exactly what they are doing. It follows that those who would protect themselves, or others, from false rumors must understand the underlying mechanisms as well. We shall see that while old-style censorship is out of the question, it is not illegitimate for courts to use libel law to protect people—whether or not in public life—from falsehoods. But part of my goal has nothing at all to do with law. It is to suggest the possibility of what social scientists call *debiasing*—in this case, through an improved understanding of how information spreads. That understanding might lead us to be more cautious in accepting false rumors, and in the process help to create a kind of culture that avoids injury or even destruction to personal lives and valuable institutions, both large and small. A well-functioning culture of free expression welcomes all comers; it makes a lot of room for speculation, for skepticism, and for dissent. But it does not welcome or encourage destruction and lies.

Propagators

Why do rumors start? Why do some rumors obtain large audiences, while other rumors fall of their own (lack of) weight? Let us begin by making some distinctions.

Rumors are often initiated by self-conscious propagators, who may or may not believe the rumors they spread. Rumor propagators have diverse motivations. To understand the current situation, we need to identify them.

Some propagators are *narrowly self-interested*. They seek to promote their own interests by harming a particular person or group. They want to make money, to win some competition, or otherwise to get ahead. They spread rumors for that reason. An allegation that Senator Jones or Secretary Smith is racist or sexist, or has been engaging in misbehavior or some corrupt project, is a common example. Similarly, investors might attempt to inflate or deflate stock prices by circulating a rumor about future events. They have invested in Orange Computers, a new company, and so they spread a rumor about its fabulous new product. Or they hate Detroit Motors, an old company, and so they spread a rumor about its coming troubles. Supporters of a particular candidate frequently insinuate that the opposing candidate has some terrible secret in his past. When members of the Republican Party spread rumors about a nominee of a Democratic president, they hope to injure not only the reputation and standing of the appointee but also those of the president and the Democratic Party as a whole, thus promoting the interests of Republicans. In fact the harm inflicted on the appointee may be beside the point—a kind of collateral damage.

11

Other propagators are *generally self-interested.* They may seek to attract readers or eyeballs by spreading rumors. In 2008 and 2009 (and even thereafter), some right-wing websites liked to make absurd and hateful remarks about the alleged relationship between Barack Obama and former 1960s radical Bill Ayers; one of the websites' goals was undoubtedly to attract more viewers. Propagators of this kind are entirely willing to publish rumors about people's professional or personal lives, and those rumors may be false. But they have no stake in hurting anyone. However serious, the damage turns out to be collateral. On the Internet, people often publish false rumors as a way of attracting eyeballs. Those who spread baseless gossip fall into this category. Their initiation of the rumor might be based on no evidence, a little, a moderate amount, or a great deal. What matters is that their self-interest is conspicuously at stake.

Still other propagators are *altruistic.* They are concerned with some kind of cause. When they say that some public person has a ridiculous or dangerous belief, or has engaged in terrible misconduct, they are attempting to promote the public good as they see it. In starting or spreading a rumor about an individual or an institution, propagators often hope to help the cause they favor. On the Internet as well as talk radio, altruistic propagators are easy to find; they play an especially large role in the political domain. When radio talk show hosts and websites attack Barack Obama because of his alleged associations, one of their goals might be to promote values and causes that they cherish.

No less than their self-interested counterparts, altruistic propagators can be unusually casual with the truth, in the sense that they are sometimes willing to say what they know to be false, and more often willing to affirm what they do not know to be true. A kind of outrage industry is easy to find on television, radio, and the Internet. One product of the outrage industry is a series of false, or at least misleading, rumors about people whose commitments are different from the commitments of those who try to spread their outrage. The key point is that those who are outraged, and who try to propagate that emotion, are often altruistic.

Finally, other propagators are *malicious*. They seek to disclose and disseminate embarrassing or damaging details, not for self-interest or to promote a cause, but simply to inflict pain. They affirmatively want to harm people, usually out of some kind of anger, rage, or perceived or real hurt, created either by particular events or by a general disposition. Here as well, the relationship between their statements and the truth may not be at all close.

Prurient, cruel, and malicious propagators will be especially effective when those who read or hear them are facing some kind of distress and when they seek to make sense out of their situation. Their actions are especially worrisome insofar as they are able to spread rumors about ordinary people who find that their reputations, their relationships, and their careers are seriously damaged. Such rumors often stick, and even if they do not, they can raise questions and doubts that haunt people for a long time.

Propagators are diverse along many dimensions, but their efforts show similar patterns. Here is an increasingly common one. In a blog post, a propagator offers an account of a person or an institution—of behavior, plans, or views. The post is read by very few, but it is there for the world to see. Other bloggers pick up the account, even if it is baseless and absurd. They do so not because they have independent reason to believe that it is true, but because they lack independent reason to believe that it is false. Perhaps they are alarmed, angry, fearful, or merely intrigued. In a relatively short time, the account appears on a significant number of blogs. At that point, hundreds, thousands, or even tens of thousands of people end up accepting the account; they are themselves alarmed, angry, or fearful. Perhaps a corrective will appear on some other blog; but perhaps it will be dismissed. In some cases, the rumor will migrate to legitimate news sources and serious questions will be asked about the person or institution. And even if the questions are silly or absurd, the very fact that questions are being asked ("Did you, in fact, commit a crime, or ally yourself with an absurd cause, or show terrible judgment?") will assure a victory for the propagator.

The Importance of Prior Convictions

When and why do rumors spread? It is clear that propagators will have an especially easy time with some groups and in some circumstances. If a group is threatened, losing, suffering, or facing difficulty, many of its members will be angry, and they will want to blame someone. Whenever a threat looms or a terrible event has occurred, rumors are inevitable. Most people are not able to know, on the basis of personal or direct knowledge, why an airplane crashed, why a leader was assassinated, why a terrorist attack succeeded, or why the economy suddenly got worse. In the aftermath of a crisis, numerous speculations will be offered. To some people, those speculations will seem plausible, perhaps because they provide a suitable outlet for outrage and blame. Terrible events produce outrage, and when people are outraged, they are all the more likely to accept rumors that justify their emotional states, and also to attribute those events to intentional action. Some rumors simultaneously relieve "a primary emotional urge" and offer an explanation, to those who accept them, of why they feel as they do; the rumor "rationalizes while it relieves."[6] And when conditions are unstable, people may be especially likely to accept a rumor about the self-serving or invidious plans of influential people.

Whether people believe a rumor may well depend on what they thought before they heard it. Suppose that you hear a damaging rumor about your best friend—say, that he has betrayed his wife or stolen money from his company. You will probably be inclined not to believe it. Now suppose that you hear a similar rumor about your least favorite public official. If the rumor fits with what you dislike about that official, you might well accept it as truth. But why? There are two reasons.

Many of our beliefs spring from our hopes, our goals, and our desires. In this sense, our beliefs are *motivated*. It makes us feel good or better to accept certain propositions, and rejecting those propositions would make us feel bad or even miserable. Suppose that you are the proud owner of a new Toyota Camry Hybrid. Suppose that you hear a rumor to the effect that the Toyota Camry Hybrid has a serious design defect and is likely to break down within two months. Your first reaction might well be: "I don't believe it!"

A great deal of work demonstrates that people try to reduce cognitive dissonance by denying claims that contradict

15

their deepest beliefs, or the beliefs that they most want to hold.[7] If propagators spread a rumor that the government of the United States has done something truly terrible, most Americans will be inclined to dismiss the rumor. For many of us, it is extremely disturbing to hear that our own government has done something reprehensible. So too, your family members are not likely to believe a false and damaging rumor about you. To reduce cognitive dissonance, we are less likely to credit rumors if we do not want to do so. It is partly for this reason that echo chambers reinforce accepted truths. When close allies of a public figure claim not to believe a damaging but apparently credible rumor about her, they might well be telling the truth; they are strongly motivated to deny the rumor not merely publicly but also to themselves.

These points help to explain why some people are immediately inclined to believe rumors that others dismiss. If the citizens of Iraq distrust the government of the United States, they will be motivated to assume the worst about that government. (Amidst difficult recent periods in Iraq, all sorts of false rumors have been widely believed. For example, some people in Iraq have thought that the U.S. military included numerous non-Americans who were enlisted in the occupation—and were killed in the war and buried in obscure places to conceal their participation.) If you are inclined to dislike some public figure or actually enjoy thinking the worst of him, you will be motivated to think that damaging rumors about him are true even if they stretch your credulity. The false rumor that Governor Sarah Palin thought that Africa was a nation rather than a continent made her critics happy. Those who disapproved of her undoubtedly enjoyed believing that she had made such an absurd blunder.

We now have an initial sense of why different groups and even nations have widely divergent reactions to rumors. Some groups and nations are strongly motivated to accept rumors that others are equally motivated to reject. The popularity of conspiracy theories can be understood in the same way. When some people believe that the 9/11 attacks were orchestrated by the United States, or that Jewish bankers are responsible for some economic disaster, it is because they like having those beliefs.

To understand the role of prior convictions, however, it is important to see that motivations are only part of the picture. Purely cognitive factors, not involving emotions, matter as well. Whether you believe a rumor will depend in part on how that rumor fits with what you already know. If a rumor cannot fit with your existing stock of knowledge, it will seem ridiculous and have no force. If Jones is one of your best friends, you have reason not to credit a rumor that he has been stealing money from his company or working to undermine his country. Having spent some time with your new Toyota Camry Hybrid and seeing how well it performs, you have reason to dismiss a rumor of its imminent breakdown. Your willingness to believe a rumor will inevitably depend on the information with which you start. (This is one reason that people are unlikely to accept damaging rumors about people and things they know well.)

We now have a different explanation of why political rumors have radically different receptions in different audiences. Those who like Senator Jones are likely to have favorable information about him, and it will take a lot of new evidence to persuade them to change their beliefs. Those who dislike Senator Jones usually have unfavorable information about him, and negative rumors will therefore find fertile territory. For this reason as well, some rumors that receive respectful attention in some groups produce incredulity, contempt, and laughter in others. Prior knowledge operates both to prevent and to fuel rumors.

In any society, people will have different "thresholds" for accepting a rumor.[8] Some might readily believe that Smith has developed a gambling problem; maybe they do not like Smith and maybe they have observed some behavior, on Smith's part, that fits with the rumor. Let us call this group "the receptives." Other people might have no inclination either way; they neither like nor dislike Smith and have little relevant knowledge. With a little evidence, or with the shared view of a few people, they might come to accept the rumor. Let us call these people "the neutrals." Still other people may like and trust Smith; they will require a great deal of corroborating information to accept the rumor. But once the evidence becomes overwhelming, they will yield. Let us call this group "the skeptics."

Within these diverse thresholds, "tipping points" can be found at which numerous people can eventually be led to accept the rumor. Suppose that propagators successfully reach the receptives. If that group is large enough, its shared conviction may eventually persuade the neutrals. And if the neutrals are numerous, some of the skeptics might begin to "tip," leading to social convergence on a new belief.

We can see the role of tipping points in many domains. For example, many people were initially reluctant to accept the claim that President Richard Nixon was actually involved in a conspiracy to hide wiretapping at the Watergate Hotel. But the receptives (those who greatly disliked President Nixon and were prepared to believe the worst about him) were fairly easily persuaded, and eventually the neutrals moved as well. Before long the shared belief of millions of Americans, together with apparently incontrovertible evidence, moved the skeptics as well.

This general process accounts for changes in beliefs of all kinds—involving, for example, religious convictions, Darwinism, the merits of political candidates, beliefs about same-sex relations, and much more. It is worth pausing over the nature of religious conversion, which often occurs in this manner. Why do some people become Christians, others Jews, others agnostics, others atheists? The shared beliefs of trusted others are exceedingly important, and tipping points matter here as well. But the underlying dynamics are especially clear with respect to rumors. (Some religious beliefs are of course based on rumors.) Let us now investigate those dynamics in more detail.

Learning from Others, 1: Informational Cascades

Rumors frequently spread through informational cascades. The basic dynamic behind such cascades is simple: once a certain number of people appear to believe a rumor, others will believe it too, unless they have good reason to believe that it is false. Most rumors involve topics on which people lack direct or personal knowledge, and so most of us defer to the crowd. As more people defer, thus making the crowd grow, there is a real risk that large groups of people will believe rumors even though they are entirely false.

Imagine a group of people who are deciding whether Senator Jones has done something scandalous.[9] Each member of the group is announcing his view in sequence. Andrew is the first to speak; perhaps he is the propagator of the rumor. Andrew states that Senator Jones has indeed done something scandalous. Barbara now knows Andrew's judgment. Exercising her own independent judgment on the basis of what she knows of the senator, she might agree with Andrew. If she has no knowledge at all about Senator Jones, she might also agree with Andrew; perhaps she accepts Andrew's claim that he knows what he is talking about. Or suppose that her independent judgment is that Senator Jones probably did not engage in the scandalous conduct. She still might believe the rumor. If she trusts Andrews no more and no less than she trusts herself, she might not know what to think or do; she might simply flip a coin.

Now consider a third person, Carl. Suppose that both Andrew and Barbara suggest that they believe the rumor, but that Carl's own information, though far from conclusive, indicates that their belief is wrong. Even in that event, Carl might well ignore what he knows and follow Andrew and Barbara. It is likely, after all, that both Andrew and Barbara had reasons for reaching their conclusion, and unless Carl thinks that his own information is better than theirs, he may follow their lead. If he does, Carl is in a cascade.

Now suppose that Carl has agreed with Andrew and Barbara; lacking any personal information about Senator

Jones, he thinks they are probably right. Suppose too that other group members—Dennis, Ellen, and Frances—know what Andrew, Barbara, and Carl think and said, and believe that their judgments are probably reasonable. In that event, they will do exactly what Carl did: accept the rumor about Senator Jones even if they have no relevant knowledge. Our little group might accept the rumor even if Andrew initially said something that he knew to be false or spoke honestly but erroneously. Andrew's initial statement, in short, can start a cascade in which a number of people accept and spread serious misinformation.

All this might seem unrealistic, but cascades often do occur in the real world. In fact, this little account helps to explain the transmission of many rumors. Even among specialists, cascades are common. Thus an article in the *New England Journal of Medicine* explores "bandwagon diseases," in which doctors act like "lemmings, episodically and with a blind infectious enthusiasm pushing certain diseases and treatments primarily because everyone else is doing the same."[10] There can be serious consequences. "Most doctors are not at the cutting edge of research; their inevitable reliance upon what colleagues have done and are doing leads to numerous surgical fads and treatment-caused illnesses."[11] Some medical practices, including tonsillectomy, "seem to have been adopted initially based on weak information," and extreme differences in tonsillectomy frequencies (and other procedures, including vaccinations) provide good evidence that cascades are at work.[12]

On the Internet, informational cascades occur every day, and even when they involve baseless rumors, they can greatly affect our beliefs and our behavior. Consider the fact that YouTube videos are far more likely to attract many more viewers if they have already attracted more viewers—a clear example of a cascade.

It is true that many cascades spread truth, and they can do a lot of good. Cascades help account for the beliefs that the earth is round, that racial segregation is wrong, that people should be allowed to engage in free speech, and that democracy is the best form of government. A bank might really be failing, and a politician might really be corrupt, and if a cascade spreads these facts, so much the better. The attack on apartheid in South Africa and the global movement for gender equality were both fueled by informational cascades. But false rumors often also set off cascades, and when they do, two major social problems occur. First and most important, people can come to believe a falsehood, possibly a damaging one. Such cascades can ruin relationships, businesses, and careers. Second, those who are in the cascade generally do not disclose their private doubts. People may have some sense that Senator Jones is unlikely to have done what he is accused of doing, but they follow the lead of those who came before them. Recall the self-interested or malicious motivations of many propagators; we can now have a better sense of why it is important to chill the falsehoods they circulate.

With respect to rumors, of course, people start with different levels of information. Many of us lack any relevant information at all. Once we hear something that seems plausible but alarming, those of us who lack information may believe what we hear if we do not know anything to the contrary. Other people are not ignorant; they do know something that is relevant, but not enough to overcome the shared beliefs of many others, at least when those others are trusted. Still other people will have a significant amount of relevant information, but are nonetheless motivated to accept the false rumor. Recall the importance of tipping points: rumors often spread through a process in which they are accepted by people with low thresholds first, and, as the number of believers swells, eventually by others with higher thresholds who conclude, not unreasonably, that so many people cannot be wrong.[13] The ultimate result is that large numbers of people end up accepting a false rumor even though it is quite baseless. The Internet provides countless case studies. A propagator makes a statement on a blog; other blogs pick up the statement; and eventually the accumulation of statements makes a real impression, certainly among people within specific social networks, and perhaps far more generally. Both truths and falsehoods spread in this fashion.

A remarkable study, not of rumors but of music downloads, is revealing on this process. The Princeton sociologist Matthew Salganik and his coauthors[14] created an artificial music market among 14,341 participants who were visitors to a website that was popular among young people. The participants were given a list of previously unknown songs from unknown bands. They were asked to listen to selections of any of the songs that interested them, to decide which songs (if any) to download, and to assign a rating to the songs they chose. About half of the participants made their decisions based on the names of the bands and the songs and their own independent judgment about the quality of the music. This was the control group. The participants outside of the control group were randomly assigned to one of eight possible subgroups. Within these subgroups, participants could see how many times each song had been downloaded. Each of these subgroups evolved on its own; participants in any particular world could see only the downloads in their own subgroups. The key question was whether people would be affected by the choices of others—and whether different music would become popular in different subgroups. What do you expect would happen? Would people be affected by the judgments and actions of others?

It turned out that people were dramatically influenced by the choices of their predecessors. In every one of the eight subgroups, people were far more likely to download songs that had been previously downloaded in significant numbers—and far less likely to download songs that had not been so popular. Most strikingly, the success of songs was highly unpredictable. The songs that did well or poorly in the control group, where people did not see other people's judgments, could perform very differently in the "social influence subgroups." In those worlds, most songs could become very popular or very unpopular, with everything depending on the choices of the first participants to download them. The identical song could be a hit or a failure, simply because other people, at the start, chose to download it or not. As Salganik and his coauthors put it: "In general, the 'best' songs never do very badly, and the 'worst' songs never do extremely well," but—and this is the remarkable point— "almost any other result is possible."[15]

In a related study, Salganik and his coauthors, acting not unlike propagators, attempted to influence the process. They told people, falsely, that certain songs had been downloaded in large numbers, even though they had actually proved unpopular.[16] More particularly, the researchers actually inverted true popularity, so that people would see the least popular songs as having the most downloads and the most popular songs the fewest. Their key finding was that they were able to produce self-fulfilling prophecies, in which false perceptions of popularity produced actual popularity over time. When people think that songs are popular, songs actually become popular, at least in the short run. True, the most popular songs did in fact recover their popularity, but it took a while, and songs that had previously been among the least popular—before the inversion—continued to be at or toward the top of the list. This is a striking demonstration of how people's behavior can be affected by an understanding, even a false one, of what other people think and do.

The music download experiments help to explain how rumors spread. Alleged facts about a politician or a country or a company do move far more in one group than in another—and in different worlds, people will believe different "facts." The variable success of rumors provides a real-world analogue to the concept, so popular in science fiction novels, of "parallel worlds." With respect to rumors, some people do seem to live in parallel worlds, even within a single nation; Republicans and Democrats sometimes seem a bit like that, with rumors taken quite seriously by one party that are dismissed by another.

Even without self-conscious efforts at manipulation, certain rumors will become entrenched in some places and have no success at all in others. If propagators are clever, they will attempt to convince people that others have come to believe the rumor that they are creating or spreading. One propagator will have terrific success in some worlds but none at all in others; another propagator will show a radically different pattern of success and failure. Quality, assessed in terms of correspondence to the truth, might not matter a great deal or even at all. Recall that on YouTube, cascades are common, as popular videos attract increasing attention not necessarily because they are good but because they are popular. Something similar happens every day on Twitter.

In light of this, we can see why some social groups hold quite tenaciously to false rumors, while other groups treat them as implausible or even ridiculous. From a few decades ago, an example was the existence of widely divergent judgments among differing groups about the origins and causes of AIDS—with some groups believing, falsely, that the first cases were observed in Africa as a result of sexual relations between human beings and monkeys, and with other groups believing, also falsely, that the virus was produced in government laboratories.[17] A more recent example is the existence of the widely divergent views about the causes of the 9/11 attacks—views that attribute the attacks to many sources, including Israel and the United States.

The multiple views about AIDS and the attacks of 9/11 are products of social interactions and in particular of informational cascades. The same process occurs when groups come to believe some alleged fact about the secret beliefs, plans, foolishness, or terrible misdeeds of a public or private figure. In each instance an informational cascade is often at work. And when cascade-propelled rumors turn into firm beliefs, the combination can be devastating. Recall that people holding similar beliefs are especially likely to accept some rumors and to discount others. Suppose that one group (in, say, Utah or Iran) has been subject to a rumor-driven cascade, while another group (in, say, New York or

Canada) has not. If so, those in the different "worlds" will develop strong prior beliefs with which they will approach whatever they hear later—beliefs that may make corrections hard to accept, a point to which I will return.

Learning from Others, 2: Conformity Cascades

Sometimes people believe rumors because other people believe them. But sometimes people just act as if they do. They censor themselves so that they can appear to agree with the crowd. Conformity pressures offer yet another insight into how rumors spread.

To see how conformity works, let us consider some classic experiments by the psychologist Solomon Asch, who explored whether people would be willing to overlook the unambiguous evidence of their own senses.[18] In these experiments, the subject was placed into a group of seven to nine people who seemed to be other subjects in the experiment but who were actually Asch's confederates. Their ridiculously simple task was to "match" a particular line, shown on a large white card, to the one of three "comparison lines" that was identical to it in length. The two nonmatching lines were substantially different, with the differential varying from an inch and three-quarters to three-quarters of an inch.

In the first two rounds of the Asch experiments, everyone agrees about the right answer. "The discriminations are simple; each individual monotonously calls out the same judgment."[19] But "suddenly this harmony is disturbed at the third round."[20] All other group members make what is obviously, to the subject and to any reasonable person, a glaring error, matching the line at issue to one that is conspicuously longer or shorter. In these circumstances, the subject has a choice: she can maintain her independent judgment or instead accept the view of the unanimous majority.

What happened? Remarkably, most people end up yielding to the group at least once in a series of trials. When asked to decide on their own, without seeing judgments from others, people erred less than 1 percent of the time. But in rounds in which group pressure supported the incorrect answer, people erred 36.8 percent of the time.[21] Indeed, in a series of twelve questions, no less than 70 percent of people went along with the group, and defied the evidence of their own senses, at least once.[22]

Why did this happen? Several conformists stated, in private interviews, that their own opinions must have been wrong—an answer suggesting that they were moved not by peer pressure but instead by a belief that the shared belief of others is probably correct. And indeed, more recent conformity studies have found that when people are exposed to the recollections of others, their own memories are materially affected, even if the recollections of others are quite erroneous. Strikingly, exposure to false recollections can result in false memories encoded in the sectors of the brain associated with long-term memory.[23] This finding suggests the possibility that when people hear the views of others, their views are genuinely altered, even if those views involve sensory perceptions.

On the other hand, experimenters using the same basic circumstances of Asch's experiments have generally found significantly reduced error when the subject is asked to give a purely private answer.[24] And when the subject knows that conformity or deviation will be easily identified, there is more conformity.[25] These findings suggest that peer pressure matters—and that it induces what the economist Timur Kuran has called *knowledge falsification*, that is, public statements in which people misrepresent their actual knowledge.[26] Here, then, is a clue to the relationship between successful rumors and conformity pressures. People will falsify their own knowledge, or at least squelch their own doubts, in the face of the apparent views of a crowd.

Rumors often spread as a result of conformity cascades, which are especially important in social networks made up of tightly knit groups or in which there is a strong stake in a certain set of beliefs. In a conformity cascade, people go along with the group in order to maintain the good opinion of others—no matter their private views and doubts. Suppose that Albert suggests that a certain political figure is corrupt and that Barbara concurs with Albert, not because she actually thinks that Albert is right, but because she does not wish to seem, to Albert, to be ignorant or indifferent to official corruption. If Albert and Barbara say that the official is corrupt, Cynthia might not contradict them publicly and might even appear to share their judgment. She does so not because she believes that judgment to be correct, but because she does not want to face their hostility or lose their good opinion.

It should be easy to see how this process might generate a special kind of cascade. Once Albert, Barbara, and Cynthia offer a united front on the issue, their friend David might be reluctant to contradict them even if he thinks that they are wrong. The apparently shared view of Albert, Barbara, and Cynthia imparts real information: that their view might be right. But even if David is skeptical or has reason to believe that they are wrong, he might not want to break with them publicly.

Conformity cascades can certainly produce convergence on truth. Maybe unduly skeptical people are silencing themselves—not the worst thing if their skepticism is baseless. But conformity cascades often help spread false rumors. Especially when people operate within a tightly knit group or live in some kind of enclave, they may silence themselves in the face of an emerging judgment or opinion even if they are not sure whether it is right. Often people will be suspicious of a rumor, or believe that it is not true, but they will not contradict the judgment of the relevant group, largely in order to avoid social sanctions. Consider far-left and far-right groups, in which well-organized social networks often spread damaging falsehoods, frequently about their real or imagined adversaries, with the aid of conformity pressures.

In the actual world, people are of course uncertain whether publicly expressed statements are a product of independent knowledge, participation in an informational cascade, or the pressure of conformity. Much of the time, we overestimate the extent to which the actions of others are based on independent information rather than social pressures. False rumors become entrenched as a result. And here too, of course, diverse thresholds matter a great deal. David may silence himself and agree with the group only when the pressure to conform is intense; Barbara might be more willing to go along with the crowd. But if most of the world consists of people like Barbara, then the Davids are more likely to eventually yield. There are tipping points for conformity no less than for information.

Learning from Others, 3: Group Polarization

Deliberation among like-minded people often entrenches false rumors.[27] The explanations here overlap with those that account for social cascades, but the dynamics are distinctive. Here again, we can understand why some groups will end up firmly believing rumors that seem ludicrous or implausible to others.

The Basic Finding

In the summer of 2005, a small experiment in democracy was held in Colorado.[28] Sixty American citizens were brought together and assembled into ten groups, each consisting of six people. Members of each group were asked to deliberate on several issues, including one of the most controversial of the day: *Should the United States sign an international treaty to combat global warming?* In order to answer that question, people had to come to terms with what were, in a sense, rumors. They had to ask whether climate change was real or instead a hoax, whether the American economy would be badly harmed by participation in an international agreement, and whether such an agreement was necessary to prevent an imminent or long-term disaster for the United States.

As the experiment was designed, the groups consisted of "liberal" and "conservative" members—the former from Boulder, the latter from Colorado Springs. In the parlance of election years, there were five "blue state" groups and five "red state" groups—five groups whose members initially tended toward liberal positions on climate change, and five whose members tended toward conservative positions on that issue. People were asked to state their opinions anonymously both before and after fifteen minutes of group discussion. What was the effect of discussion?

The results were simple. In almost every group, members ended up holding more extreme positions after they spoke with one another. Most of the liberals in Boulder favored an international treaty to control global warming before discussion; they favored it more strongly after discussion. Many of the conservatives in Colorado Springs were somewhat skeptical about that treaty before discussion; they strongly opposed it after discussion. Aside from increasing extremism, the experiment had an independent effect: it made both liberal groups and conservative groups significantly more homogeneous—and thus squelched diversity. Before their members started to talk, both the "red" and the "blue" groups displayed a fair bit of internal disagreement. The disagreements were reduced as a result of a mere fifteen-minute discussion. Even in their anonymous statements, group members showed far more consensus after discussion than before.

Moreover, the rift between liberals and conservatives widened greatly as a result of discussion. And after discussion, opinions among like-minded group members narrowed to the point where everyone mostly agreed with everyone else.

The Colorado experiment is a case study in group polarization: when like-minded people deliberate, they typically end up adopting a more extreme position in line with their predeliberation inclinations.[29] Group polarization is pervasive in human life. If a group of people tends to believe that the nation's leader is a criminal, or that some corporate executive is a scoundrel, or that one of their own members has betrayed them, their belief to this effect will be strengthened after they speak among themselves.

In the context of rumor transmission, the implication is simple. When group members begin with an antecedent belief in a rumor, internal deliberations will strengthen their belief that it is true (even if their belief was originally weak). The antecedent commitment might involve a specific claim, including a bit of gossip about an apparently powerful person. Or it might involve a more general belief with which the rumor easily fits. The key point is that internal deliberations further entrench the rumor.

The initial experiments establishing group polarization studied how social interactions would affect people's approach to risks.[30] Consider, for example, the questions whether to take a new job, to invest in a foreign country, to escape from a prisoner-of-war camp, or to run for political office.[31] When members of a group deliberated on these questions, they became significantly more disposed to take risks after a brief period of discussion with one another. On the basis of such evidence, it became standard to believe that deliberation among randomly selected people would produce a systematic "risky shift." The major consequence of group discussion, it was thought for quite a long time, was to produce that risky shift.

But later studies cast this conclusion into serious doubt. On many of the same questions on which Americans displayed a risky shift, Taiwanese subjects showed a "cautious shift."[32] On most of the topics just listed, deliberation led citizens of Taiwan to become significantly less risk-inclined than they were before they started to talk. Nor was the cautious shift limited to the Taiwanese. Among Americans, deliberation sometimes produced a cautious shift as well, as risk-averse people became more reluctant to take certain risks after they talked with one another.[33]

At first glance, it seemed hard to reconcile these competing findings, but the reconciliation turned out to be simple: *the predeliberation median is the best predictor of the direction of the shift*.[34] When group members are disposed toward risk taking, a risky shift is observed. Where members are disposed toward caution, a cautious shift is observed. It follows that the striking difference between American and Taiwanese subjects is not a product of any cultural difference with respect to how people behave in groups. It results from a difference in the predeliberation medians of the participating Americans and the participating Taiwanese on the key questions.[35] Thus the risky shift and the cautious shift are both subsumed under the general rubric of group polarization.

In the behavioral laboratory, group polarization has been shown in a remarkably wide range of contexts, many of which bear directly on transmission of rumors.[36] How good-looking is the person projected onto the screen to a group of viewers? If individuals within a group already think that the relevant person is good-looking, the entire group is likely to end up thinking that that person is devastatingly attractive.[37] (Movie stars undoubtedly benefit from this process, as do cool kids in high schools.) Group polarization also occurs for obscure factual questions, such as how far Sodom (on the Dead Sea) is below sea level.[38] Even burglars show a shift in the cautious direction when they discuss prospective criminal endeavors.[39]

In order to understand the dynamics behind rumor transmission, several studies are especially relevant. After deliberation, groups of people turn out to be far more inclined to protest apparently unfair behavior than before discussion began.[40] Consider, for example, the appropriate response to three different events: police brutality against African Americans; an apparently unjustified war; and sex discrimination by a local city council. *In every one of these contexts, deliberation made group members far more likely to support aggressive protest action.* Group members moved from support for a peaceful march to support for a nonviolent demonstration, such as a sit-in at a police station or city hall. Interestingly, the size of the shift toward a more extreme response was correlated with the initial mean. When people initially supported a strong response, group discussion produced a greater shift in the direction of support for a still-stronger response. This finding is standard within the literature: the extent of the shift is associated with the strength of the average person's starting point.[41]

When we are individually inclined to believe that unfairness has occurred, our discussions with others may well intensify our beliefs and make us very angry.[42] The most relevant studies had a high degree of realism. In one, people were asked to simulate typical office duties: budgeting items, scheduling meetings, and routing phone messages through the proper channels. Good performance could produce financial rewards. After completing the tasks, people were able to ask for their supervisors' feedback. Some of the supervisors' answers seemed rude and unfair, such as "I've decided not to read your message. The instructions say it's up to me . . . so don't bother sending me any other messages or explanations about your performance on this task" and "If you would have worked harder, then you'd have scored higher."

Participants were then asked to rate their supervisors with respect to their fairness, politeness, bias, and good leadership. First individual ratings were privately recorded; then a group consensus judgment was reached; and finally individual ratings were recorded after the group judgment. It turned out that group judgments were far more negative than the average of individual judgments.

Why Polarization?

To understand how group polarization solidifies and spreads rumors, we need to ask why like-minded people go to extremes. There are three reasons.

First, the exchange of information intensifies preexisting beliefs. People tend to respond to the arguments made by other people—and any group with some predisposition in one direction will inevitably be skewed in that direction, in the sense that the people in that group will favor, and tend to make, arguments that support what most of them think.

Suppose that you are in a group of people whose members tend to credit some rumor—that eating beef is unhealthy, that a public official has a nefarious plan, that some person did in fact engage in sexual misconduct, or that some company is about to fail. In such a group, you will hear many arguments to that effect, and considerable support for these tentative beliefs. Because of the initial distribution of views, you will hear relatively fewer opposing views. It is highly likely that you will have heard some, but not all, of the arguments that emerge from the discussion. After you have heard all of what is said, you will probably move further in the direction of thinking that eating beef is bad for you, fearing and loathing the nefarious plan, accepting the claim of sexual misconduct, and thinking that the company will fail—and you will probably be more inclined to accept supporting rumors. And even if you do not move—even if you are unusually impervious to what others think—most of your fellow group members will be affected.

Second, corroboration breeds confidence, and confidence breeds extremism. Those who lack confidence, and are unsure what they should think, tend to moderate their views.[43] Suppose that you are asked your view on some question on which you hold a tentative opinion but lack much information—say, whether a rumor involving a politician is true. You are likely to avoid an extreme position. It is for this reason that cautious people, not knowing what to do, are likely to choose the midpoint between the extremes.[44] But if other people seem to share your nascent view, you are likely to become more confident that your views are correct. As a result, you will probably move in a more extreme direction.

In a wide variety of experimental contexts, people's opinions have been shown to become more extreme simply because their initial views have been corroborated, and because they have grown confident after learning that others share their views.[45] Imagine that other people share your opinion that you can lose weight if you avoid carbohydrates, that the attacks of 9/11 were staged, or that current developments in Egypt pose a serious threat to the rest of the world. If so, your own view will be more deeply felt after you hear what they have to say.

What is especially noteworthy here is that this process—of increased confidence and increased extremism—is often occurring at roughly the same time for all participants. Suppose that a group of four people is inclined to distrust the intentions of China with respect to some international agreement. Seeing her tentative view confirmed by three others, a group member is likely to feel vindicated, to hold her view more confidently, and to move in a more extreme direction. At the same time, the very same internal movements are also occurring in *other* people (from corroboration to more confidence, and from more confidence to more extremism). But those movements may not be as visible to each participant. Most people are not carefully monitoring shifts in the views of other people, and so it will simply appear as if others "really" hold their views without hesitation. As a result, our little group might conclude, after a day's discussion, that the intentions of China cannot be trusted at all.

We have a clue here about the immense importance of social networks, online and in ordinary life, in transmitting rumors and in creating movements of various sorts. In their classic study in the 1940s, Harvard psychologists Gordon W. Allport and Leo Postman find that a necessary condition for the circulation of rumors is that "susceptible individuals must be in touch with one another."[46] Social networks can operate as polarization machines, because they help to confirm and thus amplify people's antecedent views.[47] Consider the fact that in one army camp during World War II, "the rumor that all men over thirty-five years of age were to be discharged traveled like lightning—but almost exclusively among men over that age."[48]

A far more serious example is provided by Islamic terrorism, which is fueled by spontaneous social networks, in which like-minded people spread rumors and discuss grievances, with potentially violent results.[49] Terrorism specialist Marc Sageman writes that at certain stages, "the interactivity among a 'bunch of guys' acted as an echo chamber, which progressively radicalized them to the point where they were ready to collectively join a terrorist organization. Now the same process is taking place online."[50] In Sageman's example, the major force here is not websites, which people read passively, but email lists, blogs, and discussion forums, "which are crucial in the process of radicalization."[51]

These are examples from the political domain, where false and damaging rumors run rampant; but there are many other illustrations. Why are some foods enjoyed, or rumored to be especially healthy, in some places, whereas the same foods are disliked, or rumored to be unhealthy, in other places? "Many Germans believe that drinking water after eating cherries is deadly; they also believe that putting ice in soft drinks is unhealthy. The English, however, rather enjoy a cold drink of water after some cherries; and Americans love icy refreshments."[52] In some nations, strong majorities believe that Arab terrorists were not responsible for the attacks of September 11, 2001. According to the Pew Research Center, 93 percent of Americans believe that Arab terrorists destroyed the World Trade Center, whereas only 11 percent of Kuwaitis believe that Arab terrorists destroyed the World Trade Center.[53]

A final factor is that people's concern for their reputations can increase extremism, including apparently strong commitments to false, destructive, and cruel rumors. People want to be perceived favorably by other group members, and also to perceive themselves favorably. Sometimes our views are, to a greater or lesser extent, a function of how we want to present ourselves. Of course some people are not so concerned with their self-presentation. But once we hear what others believe, many of us will adjust our positions at least slightly in the direction of the dominant position, to hold onto our preserved self-presentation. We might contain our opposition; we might voice somewhat more enthusiasm for the majority view than we really feel.

Some people might want to show, for example, that they are not likely to dismiss claims of official wrongdoing, especially in a group whose members are starting to believe a rumor about such wrongdoing. In such a group, people will frame their position so that they do not appear cowardly or cautious by comparison to other group members. And when they hear what other people think, they might find that they occupy a somewhat different position, in relation to the group, from what they hoped. They will shift accordingly. They might do so because they want others to see them in a certain way, perhaps as loyalists or cheerleaders. Or they might shift because they want to see themselves in a certain way, and a shift is necessary so that they can see themselves in the most attractive light.

The phenomenon plays a large role in the acceptance and transmission of rumors. People might endorse and even spread rumors that they do not quite believe, perhaps because it is fun and energizing to do so, perhaps to obtain social approval. Consider here some striking findings about real and apparent factual disagreements between Republicans and Democrats. Among other things, members of both parties appear to think that especially bad things (bigger budget deficits, greater unemployment) happened under presidents belonging to the political party they dislike. Sometimes Democrats and Republicans seem to live in parallel historical universes, in which the course of human events looks radically different, depending on people's political affiliations.

While a lot of research seems to support this conclusion, we now have good reason to believe that it is fundamentally wrong. Recent studies by Yale University's John Bullock and his coauthors suggest that with respect to facts, Democrats and Republicans disagree a lot less than we might think.[54] True, surveys reveal big differences. But if people are given economic rewards for giving an accurate answer, the partisan divisions start to become a lot smaller. Here's the kicker: with respect to facts, there is a real difference between what people say they believe and what they actually believe.

In their first experiment, Bullock and his colleagues asked Democrats and Republicans a series of questions and told them that for each question they answered correctly, their name would be entered into a drawing for a $200 gift certificate from Amazon.com. They were also told that the average chance of winning was 100–1, but that if they answered many questions correctly, their chances would be significantly higher. The factual questions included the change in the unemployment rate under President George W. Bush, the number of U.S. soldiers killed in Iraq from 2003 to 2011, and the percentage of the federal budget that went to the

Medicaid program. A control group was asked the same questions, but without the potential economic reward.

In the control group, the difference between Democrats and Republicans was quite large (as expected). But with the small economic incentive, the difference was cut significantly—by 55 percent. Democrats and Republicans didn't exactly come into accord, but they got a lot closer. When real money is on the line, Democrats and Republicans are far less likely to answer in a partisan fashion, and far more likely to agree with each other.

This experiment didn't allow people to answer, "I don't know." We might hypothesize that the remaining partisan division reflects a natural human reaction, which is to report a judgment that reflects your political loyalties when you just aren't sure. If this hypothesis is right, much of the apparent disagreement between Republicans and Democrats attests to people's tendency to give the benefit of the doubt to their preferred political team. Is there a way to test this hypothesis?

In their second experiment, Bullock and his colleagues did exactly that. As in the first experiment, they gave people an economic reward for a correct answer, but they also gave people a reward for a "don't know" answer. (The reward was smaller, amounting to about 25 percent of the reward for a correct answer.) Stunningly, the result was to cut partisan differences even further—to merely 20 percent of what they were in the control condition. The differences between Democrats and Republicans weren't wiped out, but they became pretty small, and hardly the stuff of real polarization across political divides.

What's going on here? When people answer factual questions about politics, they engage in a degree of cheerleading, even at the expense of the truth. In a survey setting, there is no cost to doing that. With economic incentives, of course, the calculus is altered. If you stand to earn some money with an accurate answer, cheerleading becomes much less attractive. And if you will lose real money with an inaccurate answer, you will put a higher premium on accuracy. It turns out that when Democrats and Republicans claim to disagree, they are often reporting which side they are on, not what they really think.

These points bear directly on the transmission of rumors. Often people's commitment to them is shallow, and they appear to believe them, and even repeat them, for reasons connected with loyalty and cheerleading. Rumors about misconduct, including political misconduct, are important examples here. If you hear that a public official has engaged in a stupid or corrupt project, you might signal your outrage, not necessarily because you really are outraged, but to show that you share the convictions of the group of which you are a part. One oddity is that, some of the time, group members will appear to show unswerving support for a cause, or a strong belief in a supposed fact, even though in their private moments almost all of them doubt the cause and the fact. For some people, outrage is a pleasant emotion, and disseminating a rumor that breeds outrage can enhance one's reputation, especially within certain social networks.

Biases

The discussion thus far seems to offer a simple lesson: rumors spread as a result of informational cascades and group polarization. A good solution would seem similarly simple. To correct misperceptions, steps should be taken to expose people to balanced information and to replace falsehood with truth. On the Internet, this solution seems better than ever before. Falsehoods can be spread to the world in a matter of seconds, but truths can be spread equally easily. If it is rumored that a big company is about to fail or that a certain official has a secret plan to do something awful, those who know the truth can respond immediately. But there is a serious problem with this solution. The very processes that create the false beliefs make them highly resistant to correction. Let us see why.

Human beings do not process information in a neutral way.[55] For that reason, false beliefs can be extremely difficult to correct. If we are certain that the earth is flat, that Darwin was wrong, that Barack Obama was not born in the United States, or that space aliens landed in Roswell, New Mexico, in the 1950s, we will not readily change our minds. Sometimes exposure to balanced information actually increases our commitment to our original perception.[56] Even more troublesome is the finding that the correction of false perceptions can also *increase* our commitments to those perceptions.[57] Corrections can therefore be self-defeating. If a company tries to fight a false rumor about its current difficulties, more people may end up believing the rumor. And if a person—whether a movie star or your next-door neighbor—tries to combat an Internet rumor that he has cheated on his taxes or his wife, the consequence could well be that the rumor is more widely believed.

The initial work on these points involved judgments about capital punishment and in particular about whether the death penalty deters violent crime.[58] People were asked to read several studies arguing both in favor of and against the deterrent effects of the death penalty. They also read studies offering data, critiques, and rebuttals. What would you expect would happen after people read all this information? You might predict that, having been exposed to arguments and evidence pro and con, opponents and supporters of the death penalty would move toward the middle. Perhaps opponents would see that reasonable people believe that the death penalty actually has a deterrent effect. Perhaps supporters would see that reasonable people disagree. You might expect that both groups would learn from the other side—and hence shift toward a more moderate position. If that is your prediction, you would be wrong.

A key finding was that both opponents and supporters of the death penalty were far more convinced by the studies supporting their own beliefs than by those challenging them. And after reading the opposing studies, both sides reported that their beliefs had shifted toward a stronger commitment to what they thought before they had done so. In short, exposing people to balanced information produced a more intense belief in what they had thought before—and an increase in polarization between death penalty supporters and opponents.

True, both proponents and opponents were affected, at least for a brief period of time, by reading evidence that contradicted their views. But they reverted to their original positions, or to more extreme versions of them, after reading the critiques and rebuttals. The conclusion is that when proponents and opponents of the death penalty are exposed to the same balanced evidence, the distance between their views actually increases.

This phenomenon comes with an unlovely label: biased assimilation. The simple idea is that people process information in a way that fits with their own predilections. The phenomenon has been found in many domains.[59] Consider, for example, the question whether sexual orientation has a genetic component and whether same-sex couples are able to be good parents. Confronted with both favorable and unfavorable information, the findings are clear: people's existing beliefs are fortified, and polarization on the issue of same-sex relationships increases.

For the spread of rumors, the lesson is straightforward. Suppose that members of a social group believe that the stock market is about to plummet. Suppose they encounter material that both supports and contradicts the rumor. The strong odds are that they will then end up all the more committed to their original belief. On the Internet, a process of this kind occurs every day, as those who believe rumors end up believing them all the more strongly even after hearing a balanced discussion of whether they are true. The lesson is emphatically not that balanced information cannot and will not help correct a false rumor. It is instead that in those circumstances in which biased assimilation is at work, balanced information will lead people to a stronger belief in a rumor even if it is false. I will try shortly to identify those circumstances.

Self-Defeating Corrections

When a false rumor is spreading, of course, those who are injured by it do not want balanced information. They want the falsehood to be corrected. The good news is that in many cases, corrections do succeed. In the 2008 presidential race, for example, the Obama campaign set up a website, called Fight the Smears, in which false rumors were identified and debunked. There is every reason to think that this strategy succeeded, in part because it created a kind of "poison pill." Once false rumors about then-Senator Obama were explicitly framed as "smears," they could and would be deemed unreliable for that very reason. Many other websites list Internet rumors and separate the true from the false. No systematic evidence tests their effectiveness, but it is likely that many people learn from them which rumors are false. The optimistic view emphasizes that the ease of communicating false rumors online is matched by the ease of communicating corrections.

I will return to the conditions under which the optimistic view is right, but first let us explore an important finding: corrections of false impressions can actually strengthen those very impressions.[60] Suppose there is a false but widespread rumor that Senator Johnson accepted a bribe. Suppose that the Johnson haters believe that rumor while the Johnson lovers dismiss it. Now suppose that the misperception is corrected by a credible news source. The Johnson lovers will happily take the correction as such and see the false rumor as baseless. But the Johnson haters may not be moved at all. Indeed, they might become even more convinced that their original position was right.

The most relevant experiment involving this phenomenon was conducted in 2004. Both liberals and conservatives were asked to participate in an examination of attitudes toward the existence of weapons of mass destruction in Iraq. (In fact, we now know the experiment is neatly on point, for Iraq's possession of such weapons was indeed a rumor, and a false one at that.) People read the following statement: Iraq "had an active weapons of mass destruction program, the ability to produce these weapons, and large stockpiles of WMD."[61] They were asked to state their agreement on a five-point scale, from "strongly agree" to "strongly disagree." They were then exposed to a mock news article in which President Bush defended the Iraq war, in part by suggesting (as President Bush in fact did) that there "was a risk, a real risk, that Saddam Hussein would pass weapons or materials or information to terrorist networks."[62] After reading this article, participants read about the Duelfer Report, which showed that the Bush administration was wrong to think that Iraq had weapons of mass destruction. When finished with both articles, they were again asked to state their agreement, on the five-point scale, with the original statement.

What was the effect of the Duelfer Report's correction of the original statement—that Iraq had an active WMD program—on people's belief about President Bush's assertion that Iraq could give terrorists these weapons? The answer depended on the participant's ideology. Liberals shifted in the direction of even greater disagreement with the statement. The shift was not significant, because the most liberal subjects already tended strongly to disagree with it. But for those who characterized themselves as conservative, there was a significant shift in the direction of *agreeing* with the statement. In the words of those who conducted the study, "the correction backfired—conservatives who received a correction telling them that Iraq did not have WMD were more likely to believe that Iraq had WMD."[63] Not only did the correction fail, but it had a polarizing effect; it divided people more sharply than they had been divided before.

An independent study confirmed the general effect. People were asked to evaluate the proposition that cutting taxes is so effective in stimulating economic growth that it actually increases government revenue. They were then asked to read a correction from either the *New York Times* or FoxNews.com. When they did so, the correction actually increased people's commitment to the proposition in question. Presented with evidence that tax cuts do not increase government revenues, conservatives ended up with a commitment to this belief stronger than that of conservatives who did not read a correction.

Or consider this question: does Obamacare create death panels? How do people answer this question? A careful study, with the illuminating title "The Hazards of Correcting Myths about Health Care Reform," offers some clues.[64]

One group of participants was provided with a 2009 news article in which Sarah Palin claimed that the Affordable Care Act created death panels and that these panels included bureaucrats authorized to decide whether seniors were "worthy of health care." A separate group was given the same news story, but with an appended correction saying that "nonpartisan health care experts have concluded that Palin is wrong."

The study's big question: Would the correction have any effect? Would people who saw the correction be less likely to believe that the Affordable Care Act calls for death panels? Not surprisingly, the correction was more likely to convince people who viewed Palin unfavorably than those who had a high opinion of her. Notably, the correction also tended to sway the participants who liked Palin but who didn't have a lot of political knowledge (as measured by their answers to general questions, such as how many terms a president may serve). But here's the most interesting finding in the study. Those who viewed Palin favorably, and who also had a lot of political knowledge, were not persuaded by the correction. On the contrary, it made them more likely to believe Palin was right. Remarkably, those with less political knowledge were more likely to learn from the correction—a finding with important implications for rumors, and one to which I will return.

Liberals are hardly immune to this general effect. Many liberals believe, wrongly, that President George W. Bush imposed a ban on stem cell research. Presented with a correction from either the *New York Times* or FoxNews.com, liberals continued to believe what they had before. By contrast, conservatives accepted the correction. Hence the correction produced an increase in polarization between liberals and conservatives. Notably but not surprisingly, people were affected by whether the correction came from the *New York Times* or from FoxNews.com: conservatives distrusted the former more, and liberals distrusted the latter more. It follows that the credibility of the source of the correction matters a lot—a point to which I will also return.[65]

The broader conclusion is clear. If a false rumor is circulating, efforts at correction may not help; they might even hurt. Once a cascade has spread false information or group polarization has entrenched a false belief, those who tell the truth in order to dispel the rumor may end up defeating their own goal. True, the idea of a "marketplace of ideas" does not exactly stand in tatters. But it must be acknowledged that this particular marketplace sometimes works poorly.

On Prior Convictions and Trust

How can these findings be explained? When will balanced information actually help? When do corrections work?

We have seen that when people process information, they are affected by their emotions and their prejudices. After purchasing a new tablet, people seek out more information about that very tablet. Having chosen an Amazon Kindle, they want to read more about that particular tablet. The most obvious explanation is not that they want to learn more about the tablet they have already bought. It is that they seek reassurance that they made the right decision. They are invested in that decision, emotionally as well as economically, and they want to feel good about it. Similarly, those who have voted for a particular politician may have an emotional stake in his success—and those who voted against him may have some stake in his failure. If people know a great deal, their emotional stake may be all the higher; return here to the fact that informed people can be especially immune to corrections.

Biased assimilation is partly produced by our desire to reduce cognitive dissonance.[66] We seek out and believe information that we find pleasant to learn, and we avoid and dismiss information that we find upsetting or disturbing.

51

Some rumors are fun; others are not exactly that, but they are exciting, perhaps a bit thrilling, and people enjoy believing them. Even when rumors produce outrage, people can engage them for that reason. When people are generally bitter or angry, or have a degree of background bitterness or anger, it can be comforting and even fun, in a sense, to identify grounds for outrage. Other rumors are disturbing, even a bit frightening, and people want to think that they are false.

The studies involving capital punishment and same-sex relations are best understood in this light. When people display biased assimilation, motivational factors are usually at work. If people are motivated to credit arguments that fit with what they already think and to discredit arguments that do not, the findings are unsurprising. Consider in this light what social scientists call "disconfirmation bias"—people's tendency to work especially hard to disprove arguments that contradict their original beliefs. If our judgments are motivated, then it is easy to see why balanced information might serve only to entrench our original beliefs.

But this is just part of the story. To see what is missing, suppose that society consists of two groups of people, "the Sensibles" and "the Unreasonables," and that members of both groups have strong prior beliefs. Suppose that the Sensibles have a strong commitment to certain views—say, that the Holocaust actually happened, that al-Qaeda was responsible for the attacks of 9/11, that the president is not a communist spy. Suppose that the Sensibles read balanced materials on these three questions.

To the Sensibles, the materials that support their original view will seem more than just convincing; they will also offer a range of details that, for most Sensibles, will fortify what they thought before. By contrast, the materials that contradict their original views will seem implausible, incoherent, ill-motivated, and probably a bit crazy. The result is that the original convictions of the Sensibles will be strengthened. They have learned something new in support of those convictions, and they have learned nothing at all that undermines them.

Of course the opposite pattern will be observed for the Unreasonables, who begin with the belief that the Holocaust did not happen, that the United States was itself responsible for the attacks on 9/11, that the president is a communist spy. To understand why this will be the pattern for the Unreasonables, we do not need to speak of their motivations. We can simply point to the effects of their original beliefs on how they respond to new information. Even if the Sensibles and the Unreasonables have absolutely no emotional commitment to what they think, and are simply reading what they learn in light of what they knew before, they will process the information in a biased manner. They will update their beliefs in view of what they already know. In the abstract, of course, nothing is wrong with that. If you know that your car works well, or that Senator Smith is honest, it will take a lot to convince you that your car will soon break down or that Senator Smith is corrupt. The problem arises if your antecedent beliefs make it hard or impossible for you to learn the truth.

This straightforward account helps to explain why and when biased assimilation will occur. The preconditions are twofold: strong prior beliefs and skewed trust. It follows that when people's beliefs are weak and when they trust both sides, they will learn from what they read and hear. Suppose that you do not have a strong opinion about nano-technology, and that you are informed of a rumor that this technology poses grave dangers. Suppose further that someone comes forward who provides balanced informa-tion, suggesting that the rumor is false. If you did not begin with a commitment to any particular view, your initial will-ingness to believe the rumor should soften after you are presented with balanced information. Return to the finding that people without much political knowledge were espe-cially likely to be convinced by a correction of the false claim that the Affordable Care Act creates death panels. People who do not know a lot can be open-minded. By contrast, knowledgeable people may be closed-minded, because they begin with conviction and confidence.

It also matters which sources you trust. If you like and trust Hillary Clinton, you will be inclined to accept her views on political questions. If you have a low opinion of her, you might be inclined to think that if she thinks something, it must be wrong. And if you have no idea who is propagat-ing a rumor or who is rebutting it, you will not immediately dismiss either side as biased. With respect to most rumors, of course, most of us do not have strong prior beliefs, and we do not trust one side and distrust another. These are the situations in which the marketplace of ideas is likely to work well, and in which people may well end up converging on the truth. People will listen to competing points of view and make up their minds in accordance with what they hear.

By contrast, the Sensibles and the Unreasonables trust some people and distrust others. When they read materi-als arguing both sides of an issue, it is natural that they will end up learning from the side with which they agree while discounting the other.

There is an important general lesson here. If you want people to move away from their prior convictions, and to correct a false rumor, it is best to present them not with the opinions of their usual adversaries, whom they can dismiss, but instead with the views of people with whom they closely identify.[67] Suppose that you are a Republican and you hear a devastating rumor about a Democratic official. If Democrats deny the rumor, you may not be much moved; but if Republicans do, you might well reconsider. It is no wonder that during the impeachment trial of President Bill Clinton, those opposing impeachment tried hard to find prominent Republicans, in Congress and in law schools, to state their opposition. (Interestingly, they had little success.) Nor is it surprising that in the 2008 election, the Obama campaign made excellent use of endorsements from prominent Republicans, such as former Bush secretary of state Colin Powell and former Reagan solicitor general Charles Fried. A good way to squelch a rumor is to demonstrate that those who are apt to believe it in fact do not.

55

We are now in a position to see why and when corrections are self-defeating. Suppose that the Unreasonables believe that the Holocaust did not happen and that the United States was responsible for the attacks of 9/11. After reading corrections, they may have a number of skeptical reactions. First, the correction might anger them and put them on the defensive. If so, it might produce dissonance and for that reason strengthen their (emotional) commitment to what they believed before. Second, the very existence of the correction may, for an Unreasonable, tend to confirm the truth of the original belief. Why bother to correct an error unless there is something to it? Perhaps those who purport to "correct" are protesting far too much; their protest confirms the truth of the matter that is being denied. Third, the correction may focus people's attention on the issue being debated, and the focus of their attention may itself strengthen their commitment to an existing opinion.

It is well established that when people are given information suggesting that they have no reason to fear what they previously thought to be a small risk, their fear often increases.[68] This otherwise mysterious finding is best explained by the fact that when people's attention is focused on a risk, their fear tends to go up, even if what caused them to focus on that particular risk was information that the risk was in fact small. It is scary to think about a danger, even one that is unlikely to come to fruition. People may not be so comforted to hear that they have (say) a one-in-nine-hundred chance of dying from a heart attack in the next five years, or that their child has a one-in-nine-hundred chance of developing leukemia. So too, perhaps, with corrections of false reports: by focusing people's attention on those reports, they increase the perception that what was falsely reported may in fact have occurred.[69]

We can now identify the circumstances in which corrections are not self-defeating. If those hearing the false rumor do not have strong motivations for accepting it, if they do not have a lot of prior knowledge, and if they trust those who are providing the correction, then corrections will dissipate false rumors. If any one of the three conditions is not met, corrections might well fail or even backfire. The likelihood that they will do so depends on

56

these conditions. If people are modestly motivated to accept a false rumor, if they have some (but not a lot of) prior knowledge, and if they have a moderate degree of trust in those who are providing the correction, things could go either way.

We can also see why some rumors rapidly dissipate. In the 2008 election, many of the vicious rumors about Barack Obama faded or had little impact, because most of those who heard them lacked strong prior convictions and had sufficient trust in people who came forward to correct them. Similarly, we can understand why other rumors prove tenacious. People are strongly motivated to hold them; their original convictions are firm; they do not trust those who offer corrections, which therefore turn out to be futile or counterproductive. In some communities, a rumor that white doctors spread AIDS, or that the United States was responsible for the attacks of 9/11, has real traction and can be exceedingly difficult to dislodge. In other communities, such rumors may be easily corrected. The same observation holds true for rumors involving those in the private and public spheres—and your friends and neighbors. Everything depends on motivations, prior knowledge, and trust.

It has become standard to distinguish between "dread rumors," those driven by fear, and "wish rumors," those driven by hope. The two have different relationships to the prior convictions of those who spread and accept them.[70] Many people are afraid of Islamic terrorists; when they hear a rumor of an imminent attack, they are inclined to believe it. Other people hope that an investment is about to do exceptionally well, and they are inclined to credit a rumor to that effect. Their fears and their hopes (along with their preexisting knowledge) will lead them to accept different rumors. To understand why different groups end up with different beliefs, it is important to see that one group's dread rumor may be another's wish rumor. And of course propagators who invent rumors or spread them at an early stage are often entirely aware of how relevant audiences will react. Indeed, their decisions about whether and how to spread a rumor—dread or wish—are likely to be a product of their understanding of how people will react.

An interesting twist here is that for some people, dread rumors are also, in a sense, wish rumors. If you hear that a political adversary has a nefarious secret plan, or that your least favorite senator has said or done something horrifying, you may also be gratified. Outrage can itself be gratifying, if and because it confirms our antecedent beliefs.

Note in this regard that with the rise of social media and various technologies, private surveillance of people's statements and behavior is increasingly easy. Companies may well know what you like to read and see, and from that, they may well be able to know a lot about your inclinations and your conduct. And as technologies continue to develop, propagators will have unprecedented access to what might otherwise be private information, which may be twisted into a false and damaging rumor containing a grain of truth. Jones might have said, in a bad moment, that he believes that men are better scientists than women. He does not really believe it, but he said it, and perhaps his stupid comment will appear on the Internet and help define Jones in the public eye.

Those who track your behavior on social networks may know what you said last year, or what you did last month. Taken out of context, what you said and what you did might suggest some terrible behavior or desire, or at least an error in judgment. (Like an elephant, the Internet never forgets.) And if propagators know how people will react, especially within specified social networks, they will have an increased capacity to spread their preferred rumors. If people within those networks have known fears and hopes, it should be simple to play on those fears and hopes to spread alleged facts and indeed to ensure that a belief in those allegations becomes a kind of ghost, hovering over its victim, or even that it becomes deeply entrenched. Consider candidates for public office, or presidential nominees, whose actions fifteen years ago, or whose statements ten years ago, may cause a lot of trouble, and may easily be turned into a terrible rumor of some sort.

We can now have a better sense of the circumstances that make people, groups, and nations likely to accept false rumors. Suppose that people's antecedent motivations or knowledge lead them to be especially credulous about a particular allegation. If so, falsehoods can spread rapidly, and once they are widely believed, it will be difficult to convince people to abandon those false beliefs. There is a further point, having to do with the relationship between social conditions and the spread of information. When conditions are bad, rumors, both true and false, tend to spread like wildfire. It has been observed that rumors do well "in situations characterized by social unrest. Those who undergo strain over a long period of time—victims of sustained bombings, survivors of a long epidemic, a conquered populace coping with an army of occupation, civilians grown weary of a long war, prisoners in a concentration camp, residents of neighborhoods marked by interethnic tension" are likely to believe and to spread false rumors.[71]

These are situations in which people are motivated to accept such rumors—and in which prior knowledge provides little insulation against their acceptance. Even when extreme distress is not pervasive, some people will feel angry, excluded, humiliated, aggrieved, frightened, or outraged; they will be especially susceptible to propagators. We should also be able to see that in a diverse society, some groups may suffer from strain, or relative strain, while other groups may not. Hence the conditions will be right for rumor acceptance by the former but not the latter.[72]

A noteworthy example is a tragedy that occurred in Iraq in 2005. The social stress, fear, and unrest of that war-torn region created fertile ground for false rumors. After the American invasion, the largest single-day loss of life in Iraq occurred not from a bomb, but from an informational cascade involving a false rumor. On August 31, 2005, it was widely rumored that a suicide bomb was about to go off on the Al-Aaimmah bridge, which crosses the Tigris River in Baghdad. The rumor produced a panic; the panic produced a stampede. People flocked to the bridge, and the gate opened. The pressure produced by the crowd caused the iron railings of the bridge to give way, dropping hundreds into the river. Ultimately about a thousand people were killed. This example is merely a vivid illustration of the potential consequences of informational cascades for both thought and behavior.

Emotions

To explain cascades and polarization, we can speak in purely cognitive terms. People learn from one another and care about their reputations, and propagators may succeed for those reasons alone. But we have seen that people's emotions also matter, in the sense that they are motivated to accept those rumors that fit with what they already believe. It is clear that rumors are far more likely to spread if they trigger and engage people's emotions. A purely quantitative report, noting new findings about the statistical risk of cancer associated with rising levels of arsenic in drinking water in Utah, is far less likely to attract attention than a vivid account offering scary narratives about arsenic-induced cancer deaths among children in Utah.

The most illuminating studies here demonstrate that the emotion of disgust helps to ensure that rumors spread.[73] Psychologist Chip Heath and his coauthors have found that rumors "are selected and retained in the social environment in part based on their ability to tap emotions that are common across individuals."[74] Compare, for example, these two cases: (a) Someone opened a can labeled "tuna," noticed that it smelled funny, and discovered that it was actually cat food; (b) Someone opened a can labeled "tuna," ate it, and started to feel queasy, only to discover that it was cat food. Or compare these two: (a) Before Jones drank anything from a soda, he noticed that there was a dead rat inside; (b) Jones swallowed something lumpy from a soda and saw that there were pieces of a dead rat inside. In both cases, (b) is of course more disgusting than (a). What is important is the finding by Heath and his coauthors that people reported themselves far more likely to spread the (b) rumors than the (a) rumors. Similarly, contemporary urban legends are more likely to spread on the Internet if they involve disgust. "Each additional disgust motif significantly increased the probability that a Web site would catalogue a particular legend."[75]

Heath and his coauthors contend that this process of "emotional selection" helps to explain the success of some rumors and the failure of others. Consider rumors involving satanic ritual child abuse, deviant sexual behavior, road rage, and flesh-eating bacteria. In all of these cases, emotions are likely to be triggered in a way that will increase the success of propagators. In the context of personal attacks, the parallels are evident. When rumors produce strong emotions— disgust, anger, outrage—people are far more likely to spread them. One conclusion, specifically drawn by Heath and his coauthors, is that the marketplace of ideas may well fail; the rumors that survive emotional selection "may not always be those that are most truthful."

The Surveillance Society

My topic is rumor, hardly a small subject, but the underlying concerns are even broader. Most of us want to maintain a sphere of privacy, even of secrecy, and for perfectly legitimate reasons. We want to be protected not only against false rumors, but also against disclosure of personal details that we reveal to family and close friends, not to the world. We want to ensure against disclosure of potentially embarrassing truths, and when disclosure occurs, we want to protect its extent. We make distinctions among different individuals and different groups. You might tell your best friend something that you will tell no one else; you might restrict other information to your family and closest friends. People have *circles of intimacy*, and what is disclosed within one circle will be kept from others. In the still-young era of the Internet, our desire to maintain privacy is significantly endangered. Our circles of intimacy are becoming very hard to maintain.

We can obtain an initial glance at the problem by examining a Supreme Court decision from over three decades ago.[76] A young woman—let us call her Mary Tamson—was raped. Under state law, it was a crime to disclose the name of a victim of rape unless the victim consented to the disclosure. But the police reports were not sealed, and so journalists were able to go to the police station, learn about rape cases, and report on them so long as they did not publish the victim's name. One newspaper, however, published Tamson's name in violation of the law. It contended that the First Amendment to the U.S. Constitution entitled it to do so.

The Supreme Court agreed, and so it struck down the state law. It concluded that so long as the government did not take firm steps to keep information private, journalists were entitled to broadcast that information to the world. In the Court's words, governments may not "impose sanctions on the accurate publication of the name of a rape victim obtained from public records—more specifically, from judicial records which are maintained in connection with a public prosecution and which themselves are open to public inspection."[77] The Court did not rule out the possibility that the state could seal rape cases and ban journalists from having access to any details about the victim. But the Court made it clear that once the government allowed information to be "public," it could not forbid members of the press to put that information in the newspaper or on the radio. As the Court had it, "the interests in privacy fade when the information involved already appears on the public record."

When it was originally decided in 1975, the Court's ruling seemed to announce a broad principle with large implications, to the effect that information on the public record may be published or broadcast to the world. But in the twenty-first century, the implications of this principle are far larger still. The ruling seems to suggest that if information has not been sealed, it can be put on a website and made instantly available to everyone. But is this principle a sensible one in all cases? The answer is far from obvious. In the case of rape victims, a sensible government might believe that a serious issue of privacy is involved and that unless the victim consents, her identity should not be broadcast to the world. On one view, the decision is for her to make, not the newspaper. Perhaps the government does not want to take the extreme and disturbingly undemocratic step of sealing criminal files—but it also seeks to protect the rape victim's legitimate interest in privacy by forbidding publication of her name. It is true that the First Amendment safeguards the right of free speech, and that right unquestionably includes the right to report to the public about violent crime. But is it so clear that this right includes the right to disclose the names of rape victims?

However we answer this far-from-easy question, the Court's decision signals a significant and insufficiently appreciated problem for the modern era. That problem is captured in the rise of a new kind of surveillance society. By this I do not refer to official wiretapping and government monitoring (though these can indeed be serious problems and have of course attracted considerable attention and concern). I mean instead to point to the fact that whatever your station in life, your fellow citizens are able to monitor much of what you do and much of what is done to you—and to tell the world all about it, in words, pictures, or even videos. To an increasing degree, your silly, confused, flirtatious, angry, and offensive moments, on Facebook or YouTube or Twitter or email or in daily life, are subject to being recorded and stored (forever) and, potentially, mischaracterized. At one or another time, those moments may come back to haunt you and perhaps seriously injure you.

There is an additional twist. The problem is not simply the ease with which information can now be broadcast, but also a new power for the mischievous or the malicious: to make deliberate use of all or only a part of available information to generate and encourage a false or misleading impression. It is now child's play to provide a selective broadcast of complex information and to manipulate isolated bits of data, or lives, or policies, in order to convey a deceptive or destructive sense of a person or a situation. In fact this has become a standard tool on talk radio and late-night television. True, it produces entertaining and memorable shows. Recall that outrage can be fun, in part because it makes the person who experiences it feel superior to the person who has caused it. But these kinds of context-free excerpts can be ridiculously unfair to people, and they can badly damage public discussion as well.

Perhaps a corporate executive said something, once, about the overriding importance of pursuing "profit above all" in a speech or a board meeting, and perhaps that statement can be taken out of context to suggest a kind of unprincipled pursuit of money. But perhaps the executive's real views are sensible and measured, and perhaps the snippet gives a wildly false impression of the reality. Or perhaps a mayor, or a candidate for the House of Representatives, once expressed a view—against, say, immigration reform— that reflected what she had recently read, but that now appears to her to have been mistaken. Perhaps the statement, taken out of context, can give a false impression that she is indifferent to people who are really struggling. If a cascade occurs, that single statement can easily come to define her in the public eye.

In an electoral democracy, in which frank discussion about actual and prospective public officials is essential, this is a genuine problem. The Internet is full of reports about what people (supposedly) did and said and about what they (supposedly) believe. Sometimes those reports are outright fictions based on nothing at all—reflecting only the propagator's desire to gain attention or to promote or defeat a person or cause. Sometimes those reports are not exactly false, because they are based on a shred or a kernel of truth. On a single occasion, Senator Winston may have become enraged at a staff member and behaved inappropriately, and this incident might be taken to suggest that Senator Winston has a serious anger management problem, or is even abusive. On a single occasion, Representative Johnson may have said something that suggests racism or sexism, or some kind of extremism, and his statement might seem to reveal that he is unqualified for public office. Taking incidents out of context, propagators can produce a palpably incorrect impression, one that harms not only individual people but also institutions that might benefit from their participation.

Because our lives consist of an endless number of statements and actions, it would be a most unusual person who has not, in the last decade, said or done something that, if isolated and broadcast to the world, would seem objectionable or worse. Over the course of our lives, it is nearly inevitable that all of us will make or have made statements or engaged in behavior that will seem to some members of the public a kind of smoking gun—proof of poor judgment or some kind of bad tendency or character defect. Perhaps you got drunk and behaved terribly at one party, after behaving impeccably at hundreds of parties; perhaps you made an offensive choice at a costume party, dressing up as a Nazi (as Prince Harry in fact did). One of the great risks of the era of Facebook and bloggers and YouTube is that our statements and actions can be not only stored forever but also so closely monitored that any particular one, taken out of context, will seem, or be made to seem, representative of the whole, or a clue to something dark and alarming.

To specify the concern, imagine a world, not so very different from what seems to be emerging in our own, in which our lives are monitored and filmed, not by government, but by technologies used by our peers. In a not unimaginably distant future, Google, or someone else, might be able to record every moment of every day on the planet, broadcast them live, and store all those moments for posterity. Of course recording would present serious risks to individual privacy.[78] But privacy is not the only concern. A real problem, in any such world, is that a single incident or episode could obtain real salience. And if this is so, the processes that I have described can greatly magnify that salience. Cascade effects and polarization can ensure that whole networks of people, or even large populations, learn about an incident and take it to be representative of an entire character or life. But learning about a particular incident, misleading when taken out of context, is hardly a full description of the risk. Large or immense audiences can be manipulated to believe things that, whether or not literally false, are not exactly true.

I have said that for public figures and members of public institutions, this is a serious problem. It is also a problem for self-government insofar as citizens obtain a false understanding of their actual and potential leaders. To the extent that the information society breeds misinformation, serious choices might be made on the basis of falsehoods.

There is a problem too for ordinary people. Any one of us is at risk of injury from publicity that is unwanted, misleading, unfair, or all of the above. The risk is not exactly new, but with the rise of the Internet, it has become far easier for us to wound others and to be wounded. Friends, employers, and even family members might well encounter, or be sent, a single statement you made or act you committed, and ultimately reach, or be led to reach, a damaging conclusion. Here too, that statement may well come to be taken as representative of some whole. The Internet has dramatically lowered the barriers to those who would cause such harm.

The late and not-much-lamented Office of Independent Counsel provides a way to understand this concern. After the Watergate scandal, Congress enacted the Independent Counsel Act, which permitted the attorney general to appoint an independent counsel to investigate alleged wrongdoing by specific public officials. Though unquestionably well-motivated, the Independent Counsel Act turned out to be a complete disaster—a recipe for distortions and unfairness. The reason is that most prosecutors have a limited budget and a large number of potential targets, and hence they must exercise discretion. Balancing an array of factors, they do not bring criminal charges in every case. Prosecutorial discretion, as it is called, turns out to be an important guarantee of liberty. Of course criminal acts are not acceptable. But if every criminal act resulted in a criminal prosecution, far too many people would be hiring lawyers and facing jail sentences. The Independent Counsel Act failed in large part because the independent counsel had a single target and an effectively unlimited budget. In short, the independent counsel faced excessive incentives to investigate and then to investigate some more—and if at all possible, to initiate criminal proceedings.

Compare the surveillance society in this light. The worry is not that your entire life may be reviewable on Facebook or YouTube or their successors. It is that when parts of a life are displayed in sixty-second segments, there is a serious danger that one or another moment will impose real damage on you. In light of what we know about the transmission of false rumors, we can go one step further. One foolish or aberrant act, widely broadcast, can stand in the way of those who would attempt to make a fair evaluation of your character and your life. But what of those who have no desire to make such a fair evaluation? What of those who have an active reason to ensure there is no such fair evaluation? In short, what of malicious propagators?

In democratic politics and constitutional law, the metaphor of a "marketplace of ideas" plays a central role. If free expression is permitted, the basic claim goes, a large number of arguments, interpretations, and ideas will be aired, and in the end the truth will emerge victorious. Of course we might question the very idea of a "marketplace" for ideas. There are markets for shoes, automobiles, and hotel rooms, and competition in each of these markets frequently does benefit consumers, with the best products surviving at the most reasonable prices. But in what sense, exactly, is there a market for ideas?

The answer is not entirely clear. Certainly it does not operate in the same way as does the market for shoes. There is no price system for points of view; no such system aggregates diverse knowledge and values. Acknowledging this point, we might nonetheless note that there is a highly competitive media market, with countless outlets, and we might have sympathy for the belief that the truth will frequently prevail, at least in the long run, when people have access to numerous ideas and arguments—about policies, about science, about who did what. The optimistic view—that the marketplace of ideas is essentially reliable—played a large and salutary role in twentieth-century constitutional law.

But an understanding of the mechanisms for the propagation of rumors, particularly false ones, raises doubts about this view. Even when competition among ideas is robust, terrible ideas and falsehoods can become widely accepted. Racial segregation was a bad idea, but it survived for a long time, and many people accepted it, even with a system of free speech. In the United States, discrimination on the basis of sex was both constitutional and pervasive at least until the 1970s (of course it has hardly gone away), and it was widely thought legitimate, despite a robust marketplace of ideas. If we attend to cascade effects, group polarization, and biased assimilation, we can see that even for judgments of fact, misperceptions are highly likely. Millions of Americans have believed false rumors of many different kinds. And because the Internet allows the transmission of apparently credible falsehoods within a matter of seconds, it is likely to ensure that misperceptions, including highly damaging ones, will increase over time.

With respect to acceptance of false rumors, the pessimistic view holds that many of us follow a simple rule: people generally do not say things unless they are true, or at least substantially true. If it is rumored that some student or professor engaged in some terrible misconduct, or that a candidate for public office is corrupt, many people will think that the rumor would not have gotten started unless it had some basis in fact. On this view, there is fire wherever there is smoke. And even if most of us are not so credulous, and do not adhere to such a rule, the presence of the rumor can leave a cloud of suspicion, a kind of negative feeling or after-effect that can ultimately affect our beliefs and behavior. The social influences I have sketched here help to explain the ground for the pessimistic view: if people are listening only selectively to one another, and occasionally living in echo chambers, widespread acceptance of false rumors is inevitable.

But there are two reasons to think that such pessimism might be unwarranted. The first reason is that while it is now easier than ever before to spread false rumors, we have seen that it is equally easy to produce instant corrections. A political figure is able to respond to false rumors and to reach numerous people in doing so. Recall the Obama campaign website, Fight the Smears. Even a private person, lacking any kind of celebrity, has the technical capacity to do the same thing. Each of us can fight the smears. The marketplace of ideas might be thought likely to function especially well in the modern era, precisely because it is so easy to reach so many people so quickly.

The second reason involves people's eventual reactions to the sheer proliferation of rumors, most of which are palpably false. With so much falsity, even absurdity, perhaps people will increasingly discount and distrust what they read and hear.[79] Certain Internet scams were far more effective when they started than they are today. When you read that you have won a $100 million lottery, or that someone in Kenya has inherited $524 million dollars and wants to share his bounty with you, you are not so likely to believe it, even if a decade before, you might have briefly thought, "Maybe?" The culture seems to be moving toward greater skepticism, especially when the Internet ensures that propagators can easily reach a large audience. Perhaps the generation growing up with online social networks, and that generation's successors, will treat a wide range of false rumors, including negative or even vicious ones, with bemusement, a laugh, or a yawn.

These points have some force, and they cannot easily be shown to be false; but in my view, it is doubtful that they will provide an adequate solution to the problems posed by false rumors. It is true that corrections can be made immediately, but how many people believe those corrections? Often the truth fails to catch up with a lie. In a world with cascade effects, group polarization, and biased assimilation, denials, let alone corrections, will sometimes prove ineffective. Some people will think: Why would he deny it, if it weren't true? As the slogan goes: "Never believe anything until it has been officially denied." We have already seen that corrections can be self-defeating. There is simply not enough evidence to justify the optimistic conclusion that false rumors on the Internet are adequately countered by the truth.

The claim about increasing public skepticism is more intriguing. Many of us have learned not to believe what we read on email or the Internet, even if we might have believed it some years ago. Those in authoritarian states tend not to believe their leaders; those in democratic nations take commercial advertisements with many grains of salt. We could certainly imagine a world, sometime in the future, in which most people would be quite skeptical of rumors, especially when they came from the Internet. Perhaps the very pervasiveness of false charges on the Internet, and the anonymity, bias, evident self-interest, or unreliability of many propagators, will lead people to conclude that an accusation or statement of fact on the Internet is usually a reason not for belief, but for skepticism and uncertainty.

This prediction is not self-evidently wrong, and we do seem to be in the midst of a period of cultural transition, in which many of us dismiss certain sorts of false rumors about (say) movie stars and politicians. But I suspect that the optimistic prediction underestimates the natural human tendency to believe what we hear, and also overestimates people's ability to adjust their judgments to the new world of the Internet. Even if false rumors are everywhere, we are inclined to suspect that they contain a glimmer of truth, especially when they fit with, and support, what we already believe. True, a higher dose of skepticism is a likely consequence of a world with so many unreliable voices. But even in such a world, propagators of false rumors will have many successes.

The Chilling Effect

We hardly need to imagine a world, however, in which people and institutions are being harmed by the rapid spread of damaging falsehoods via the Internet. We live in that world. What might be done to reduce the harm?

In the United States and many other nations, the law has long attempted to balance the interest in reputation with the interest in free speech. When lawyers and judges discuss that balance, they usually speak of, and deplore, the "chilling effect" that is created by the prospect of civil or criminal penalties for any speech.[80] Fearing the threat of lawsuits, whistleblowers, experts, journalists, and bloggers might keep their opinions to themselves. We should not want to discourage questions, objections, and dissent, which can promote accountability and uncover error or corruption. Strict libel laws, for example, can chill speech about public figures and public issues in a way that could damage democratic debate. And to the degree that there is something like a "marketplace of ideas," we should be especially concerned about the chilling effect, because it will undermine processes that ultimately produce the truth.

Without question, a chilling effect on freely expressed ideas can be exceedingly harmful. And without question, it is important to devise methods to reduce the risk of such harm. A free society needs to allow considerable breathing space for speakers. But let us be careful about an undue emphasis on only one side of the equation. There are two points here. *First*, we should be able to agree that on occasion, the chilling effect is a very good thing, certainly if it comes from social norms that encourage truth telling and that discourage lies. The chilling effect can reduce damaging and destructive falsehoods, including falsehoods about individuals, whether or not famous, and institutions, whether public or private. True, some falsehoods are helpful ways of producing the truth in the long run. But many false rumors are not merely damaging but also entirely useless to those who seek to know what is true. *Second*, an appreciation of the empirical evidence strongly suggests that the marketplace of ideas can fail, at least when social influences and biased assimilation ensure that false rumors spread and become entrenched. We have seen that under certain conditions, dislodging those false rumors can be exceptionally difficult.

A society without any chilling effect imposed by social norms and by law would be a singularly ugly place. What societies need is not the absence of "chill," but an optimal level. The question is: How do we get there?

Law

Current constitutional law offers one possible route. The basic principles are laid down in *New York Times Co. v.*

Sullivan,[81] one of the Supreme Court's most important decisions. The facts of the case were simple. In the early 1960s, civil rights organizations ran an advertisement in the *New York Times* complaining of brutal police responses to civil rights protests in Montgomery, Alabama. L. B. Sullivan, a Montgomery commissioner with authority over the police, brought a suit for libel.

The Supreme Court ruled that when a public official is involved, the Constitution allows recovery only if the speaker had "actual malice." This is a highly speech-protective standard. It means that speakers can be free from fear of a damage action unless (a) they are actually aware that the statement was false or (b) they acted "with reckless indifference" to the question of truth or falsity. It follows that a speaker cannot be held liable if he has spread falsehoods innocently and in good faith, or even if he acted unreasonably in saying what he did, in the sense that he had reason to know that what he was saying was false.

In explaining its conclusions, the Court stressed that the Constitution limits the government's power even when the government is attempting to control unquestionably false statements. In words that bear directly on rumors, the Court said that "erroneous statement is inevitable in free debate," and "it must be protected if the freedoms of expression are to have the 'breathing space' that they 'need to survive.'"[82] Thus neither "factual error" nor "defamatory content" is enough to remove the constitutional protection accorded to "criticism of official conduct." The Court emphasized that the free speech principle broadly protects speech that bears on public affairs. It concluded that serious constitutional limits must be imposed on civil damage awards against libelous statements, allowing those who have been libeled to recover only when they could establish "actual malice."

For public officials, the Court ruled two approaches out of bounds. It said that "strict liability," meaning liability without fault, is constitutionally unacceptable. Under the First Amendment, speakers cannot be held liable simply because they spread falsehoods. The Court also ruled out the negligence standard for public officials, even though that standard is common in most domains of the law. Suppose that your car turns out to be defective and injures you; suppose too that the manufacturer of the car was negligent in the sense that it did not use appropriate care. If so, you can recover damages to compensate for your injury. But under the Constitution, this is not true for libelous speech. Imagine that a falsehood seriously injures a public official and that the speaker should have known (in light of the evidence she had) that she was speaking falsely. Even if so, the newspaper publishing the falsehood is free from liability so long as it did not know that the statement was false and so long as it was not "recklessly indifferent" to the question of truth or falsity.

To understand the Supreme Court's ruling, it is important to see that there is a real difference between the merely negligent and the reckless. Negligence means a failure to show the appropriate standard of care; recklessness means a kind of willful refusal to consider the evidence. Many reporters are negligent; many fewer are actually reckless. If a public official can recover damages only when a speaker has been reckless, journalists of all stripes will usually be able to proceed with impunity, whatever they end up saying, and whatever the evidence ultimately reveals. It is exceedingly hard to prove recklessness, and a lawsuit is both expensive and time-consuming. Unless the case is airtight, most people in the public eye will ask: Why bother? For their part, speakers can rest assured that they can say what they want with impunity—which is generally good, in a system committed to freedom of expression, but which is sometimes harmful to both individuals and society as a whole.

Because *New York Times Co. v. Sullivan* involved public officials, it left some key questions open. What if someone libels a private individual, someone who lacks fame or notoriety? What if a newspaper publishes some damaging falsehood about Joe Smith, accusing him of corruption, bribery, theft, or other misconduct? Under long-standing principles in Anglo-American law, Smith may recover damages, and he need not even establish fault. The very facts of falsehood and harm are enough to give Smith a right to sue. The Court's analysis in *New York Times Co. v. Sullivan*, focusing on the need for "breathing space" in the context of "criticism of official conduct," did not by itself raise doubts about Smith's ability to invoke the courts to

protect his reputation.

Nonetheless, the Court eventually concluded that the free speech principle imposes restrictions on Smith's libel action too—a conclusion that has implications for what is said on Facebook, YouTube, and anywhere else. In *Gertz v. Robert Welch, Inc.*,[83] the Court ruled that people could recover damages for libel only if they could prove negligence. What this means is that if someone says something false and damaging about you, it is not enough that the statement was false and that you were badly harmed. You must also show that the speaker did not exercise proper care.

While it is exceedingly difficult to prove "actual malice," it is also not easy to establish negligence. Suppose that a reporter learns, from an apparently credible source, that a lawyer or a banker has engaged in some corrupt conduct, or that a high school teacher was sexually involved with a student. Suppose that the allegation is false. Perhaps the reporter can be deemed negligent for failing to ensure that his source was right or for failing to ask alternative sources. But it will not be easy for Smith to demonstrate that the reporter was negligent as a matter of law.

To explain its controversial conclusion in *Gertz*, the Court said that free speech "requires that we protect some falsehood in order to protect speech that matters."[84] The Court contended that a "defense for erroneous statements honestly made" is "essential." The reason is that "a rule compelling the critic of official conduct to guarantee the truth of all his factual assertions—and to do so on pain of libel judgments virtually unlimited in amount—leads to . . . 'self-censorship.'" A constitutional ban on liability without fault, along with a requirement that negligence be shown, operates as a safeguard against journalistic or speaker self-silencing. In short, the Court continued the enterprise, started in *New York Times Co. v. Sullivan*, of attempting to regulate the extent of the "chill" on free speech.

To come to terms with these conclusions, we need to make some distinctions. Some false statements involve public officials. Others involve celebrities—movie stars or dancers or singers, whose connection to the domain of self-government is obscure. Still others involve not public officials, but public issues—as, for example, when an ordinary person is accused of attempting to bribe an important executive at a local bank. And then there are those that involve ordinary people engaged in the business of ordinary life.

For those who fall within each of these categories, the law is generally clear. Public figures cannot recover for libel unless they can show actual malice. Celebrities are treated the same as public officials. Public issues are not given any kind of special status; the question turns on the status of the person who is bringing suit. Ordinary people must show negligence.

Do these rules strike the right balance? The answer is not clear. Consider those involved in public life: because actual malice is so difficult to establish, good people are subject to real damage, and those who do the damage cannot be held accountable. The problem is not restricted to those who are damaged; it extends to self-government itself, which suffers if citizens cannot make fair evaluations. Consider entertainers: those who have decided to act or to sing are at increased risk of public ridicule or even cruelty, even if they have absolutely no role in politics. Consider ordinary people: it is not easy to demonstrate negligence, and if people spread a false and damaging rumor about you, it will be difficult for you to hold them accountable. The question of compensation is less important than the question of deterrence. With the law as it now stands, most false rumors simply cannot be deterred.

Is this ideal, or even acceptable, from the standpoint of the marketplace of ideas? Do we really want to allow people to be able to spread negligent falsehoods about movie stars? True, famous people have a distinctive ability to reach large audiences and thus to correct errors, but among many viewers and readers, the truth will not prevail. Is it so important to provide breathing space for damaging falsehoods about entertainers? In any case, is it clear that ordinary people should not be able to sue when they have been harmed by falsehoods? Any marketplace requires standards and ground rules; no market can operate as a free-for-all. It is not obvious that the current regulatory system for free speech—the current setting of chill—is the one that we would or should choose for the Internet era.

I do not mean to answer these questions here. It may well be too late to suggest a fundamental rethinking of basic principles. But it is hardly too late to adapt those principles to the modern era. Part of what has motivated the Supreme Court has been a legitimate concern about high damage awards. If the law could find ways to protect people against falsehoods without producing the excessive deterrence that comes from costly lawsuits, we might be able to accommodate the conflicting interests. Consider, then, three modest ideas, ventured tentatively in an effort to bring an understanding of rumor transmission into better contact with legal requirements.

- There might be a general right to demand retraction after a clear demonstration that a statement is both false and damaging—in other words, libelous. If a newspaper or broadcaster or blogger refuses to provide a prominent retraction after a reasonable period of time, it might be liable for at least modest or nominal damages.
- On the Internet in particular, people might have a right to "notice and take down." Under this approach, modeled on the copyright provisions of the Digital Millennium Copyright Act, those who run websites would be

obliged to take down falsehoods upon notice. It is true that this approach might be burdensome—a point that argues against it. It is also true that because of the nature of the Internet, notice and takedown cannot provide a complete solution. Once material is posted, it might effectively be there forever. But if it is taken down, it will not be in quite so many places, and at least the victim of the falsehood will be able to say that it was taken down.

- Damage caps and schedules could do a great deal to promote free speech values while also ensuring a measure of deterrence. Suppose, for example, that libel awards were usually bounded at $15,000, or that steps were taken to ensure that high awards could not be imposed on defendants with limited resources. After all, speakers have reputations to protect as well. If they are subject to liability, and if it is determined that they did not tell the truth, their reputations will suffer. From the standpoint of the system of freedom of expression, speakers' concern for their reputations is not exactly a disaster; from the standpoint of ensuring against harms to individuals, it is an extremely good thing. A cap on damages, alongside liability to establish what is actually true, could work to leverage the propagator's concern for his reputation to good effect.

Before we embrace any of these proposals, we would of course be required to undertake some sustained analysis, above all of the likely consequences. I refer to them not at all to offer a final verdict, or to endorse any of them in particular, but to sketch some possible approaches that might

protect the legitimate rights of speakers while offering safeguards not only to those whose reputations might be damaged by falsehoods, but also to the many others who are
harmed when they are misinformed about people, places,
and things.

Privacy

Some rumors are not false, but they invade individual privacy. Here too, the Supreme Court has imposed constraints.
Time, Inc. v. Hill[85] involved a suit by James Hill, his wife, and
his five children, who had been held captive in their home
by three escaped convicts. A play based on the ordeal was
written, and *Life* magazine published an article about the
play; the article said that the family had been treated vio-
lently, which was false. A jury awarded the family $30,000 in
compensatory damages. The Supreme Court refused to allow
the award to stand. It said that in a case involving matters of
public interest, "sanctions against either innocent or negligent misstatement would present a grave hazard of discour-
aging the press from exercising the constitutional guarantees. Those guarantees are not for the benefit of the press so
much as for the benefit of all of us." Thus penalties could be
acceptable "only on a finding of knowing or reckless falsity."

The Court's ruling does impose serious obstacles to those
who aim to prevent intrusions on privacy, but it is important to see that the Court proceeded quite narrowly, limit-
ing itself to a particular set of facts. Consider the following
situations:

83

- Suppose that a newspaper or a blogger takes some personal event involving you and distorts it badly, thus embarrassing and injuring you. If the underlying issue is not one of public concern, the Court's ruling leaves open the possibility that the newspapers or bloggers who cast events in your life in a false light could be held liable for negligence, even if they acted in good faith. The Court has not ruled on the question of whether it is permissible for states to allow you to sue for compensation.

- The situation changes if you are a public figure. The Court did not speak directly to the question of invasions of privacy, but for public figures, and especially those involved in the political domain, the First Amendment imposes real restrictions. Courts have come close to saying that public figures essentially lose their ability to protect themselves against disclosure of private facts.[86] If a blogger or a newspaper discloses some embarrassing or even humiliating truth about a governor or a senator, the Constitution protects its right to do so.

- Insofar as we are dealing with the publication of private facts about ordinary people, the free speech principle is not yet a barrier. If a blogger or photographer invades your privacy by disclosing something that is true but highly personal, the Constitution does not forbid courts to award you compensation. True, the Internet is exceedingly difficult to control, especially with so many anonymous writers, but it remains possible for people to sue those who disclose personal details, at least if those people are not public figures.[87]

The All-Important Section 230: A Very Brief Note

Under section 230 of the Communications Decency Act, those who operate websites have immunity from liability for comments, including libelous comments, left by others. The act states, in relevant part, "No provider or user of an interactive computer service shall be treated as the publisher or speaker of any information provided by another information content provider." This provision has been interpreted to mean that Internet service providers cannot be held liable for legal wrongs committed by their users.[88]

In the key case, an America Online bulletin board contained a message with an advertisement for the sale of shirts displaying offensive statements about the Oklahoma City bombing. Kenneth Zeran, the plaintiff, had not posted the message and indeed had no connection with it; but his home phone number was posted in the message. He received a number of angry phone calls and repeatedly complained to AOL, asking it to remove his association to the offending message. AOL delayed in responding to Zeran's request, and Zeran brought suit. In the crucial passage, the court responded that section 230 "plainly immunizes computer service providers [against] . . . liability for information that originates with third parties."

Whether or not this is the right interpretation of section 230, the implications are clear: if an operator of a website, including a blogger, allows libelous material to appear and does nothing to take it down, she is at no risk of liability. In light of what we know about false rumors, reasonable people might wonder whether this is the right rule. To be sure, many service providers allow writing by large numbers of people, and it would impose a considerable burden to ask them to screen those writings. The consequence of liability—at least if it included significant damage awards—might be an unacceptable burden on freedom of speech. But is notice and takedown clearly wrong? What would be so terrible about a requirement that people take down libelous material after they are given notice that it is libelous—at least if they do not have reason to believe that the material is accurate or supported by evidence?

I have spent considerable time on legal rules, and these are unquestionably important. But in the domain of rumor transmission, culture and social norms probably matter even more. Everything depends on what propagators do and on how they are received. We could imagine a future in which propagators—whether self-interested, altruistic, or malicious—are rewarded, directly or indirectly, for spreading false rumors and for showing no concern for the question of truth; in which cascade effects and polarization ensure that countless people believe those falsehoods; and in which biased assimilation ensures that many baseless beliefs are impervious to change. In such a future, people's beliefs are a product of social networks working as echo chambers in which rumors spread like wildfire. In such a future, people are especially likely to believe claims that originate, or at least appear to originate, within their particular group and that fit with their own wishes, fears, and inclinations. In such a world, people are entirely willing to accept rumors that cast others in a terrible light, especially when those others are, or are easily seen as, adversaries.

By contrast, we could also imagine a future in which those who spread false rumors are categorized as such and marginalized; in which cascade effects are blocked by individuals or groups who think independently; in which group polarization is contained by a broad social awareness of that very phenomenon; and in which people, humble and aware of their own fallibility, are more open to the truth. In such a future, people would be fully alert to the fact that for both the most and the least powerful, false rumors threaten to be part of the stuff of daily life. Of course they listen to rumors, but they view them with a degree of distance and scrutiny, seeing their appearance on the Internet as akin to their appearance in tabloid magazines. In such a future, people approach rumors skeptically even when they provide comfort and fit with their own biases and predilections.

The choice between these futures is our own.

A Brief Recapitulation

Sensible people believe rumors, whether or not they are true. On the Internet, self-interested, malicious, and altruistic propagators find it increasingly easy to spread rumors about prominent people and institutions. Such rumors cast doubt on their target's honesty, decency, fairness, patriotism, and sometimes even sanity; often they portray public figures as fundamentally confused or corrupt. Those who are not in the public sphere are similarly vulnerable. In a matter of seconds, it is easy to portray almost anyone as guilty of poor judgment or some wrongful act, and in that sense to injure or even destroy his reputation. The Internet allows information to be provided to the world in an instant, and it allows anyone to discover that information in an instant.

The success or failure of rumors depends in large part on people's original convictions. Many of us are predisposed to accept certain damaging statements about public officials or important institutions. Accepting the truth of such statements may provide a kind of emotional relief, or may support our initial inclinations and in that sense reduce dissonance or otherwise fit with our desires. Other people, favorably disposed toward those people and institutions, are predisposed to reject the same statements simply because they produce discomfort or dissonance.

This point about motivations is complemented by one about cognition. When we begin with an initial view, it is usually because of what we know. If a rumor fits well with what we already believe, we have some reason to conclude that it is true. If the rumor is wildly inconsistent with our existing knowledge, we have some reason not to credit it. Different people and groups will have different thresholds for accepting beliefs that fit poorly with their existing motivations and knowledge; they will accept those jarring beliefs, but only after they have been given very good reason to do so. One reason involves the shared beliefs of other people, especially if they are trusted, numerous, or both. Because people start with different judgments, and have different thresholds for changing them, we can find stable commitments to certain beliefs within some groups of sensible people alongside stable commitments to sharply opposing beliefs in other groups of equally sensible people. Some of those beliefs will be groundless notwithstanding their entrenched support.

Rumor transmission frequently occurs as a result of cascade effects and group polarization. Indeed, rumors spread as a textbook example of an informational cascade: imperfectly or entirely uninformed people accept a rumor that they hear from others, and as more and more people accept that rumor, the informational signal becomes very strong, and it is hard for the rest of us to resist it, even if it is false. Sometimes conformity cascades are involved as well, as people appear to accept rumors, not because they actually believe them, but in order to curry favor with others. In closely knit communities, false rumors can become entrenched, above all because people do not want to face social sanctions. Group polarization also plays a large role, as people strengthen their commitment to a rumor simply because of discussions with like-minded others. When employers come to believe something about an employee, or teachers about a student, or students about a teacher, or voters about a public official, group polarization is typically at work.

It is tempting, in this light, to think that balanced information and unambiguous corrections can counteract false rumors. This plausible thought should be taken with many grains of salt. If people are strongly committed to a rumor, and if they distrust those who deny it, they might not be much moved by the denial. The phenomenon of biased assimilation means that a reasonable debate can strengthen an unreasonable position and increase polarization. Even more strikingly, corrections can turn out to be self-defeating in the sense that they might strengthen people's commitment to their misperception. Here as well, strong prior convictions and skewed trust are crucial. When people begin by believing a rumor, and do not trust those who try to dislodge it, corrections are not so helpful. If they are to be offered, the messenger should be someone who is taken to be especially reliable by those who accept the rumor.

It is also tempting to think that in the modern era, the ease of rebutting falsehoods, and our increasing skepticism about formal and informal sources of news and information, will operate as a safeguard against acceptance of false rumors. To date, we lack empirical evidence, but this hopeful thought is probably too optimistic. It is true that freedom of speech is a crucially important value and that the risk of a chilling effect has to be taken very seriously. It is also true that on the Internet, you can try to correct a false rumor in an instant. But even in the modern era, the marketplace of ideas can fail to produce truth; the social mechanisms explored here ensure that any marketplace will lead many people to accept destructive falsehoods.

In extreme cases, such falsehoods can create contempt, fear, hatred, and even violence. Some kind of chilling effect on the damaging effects of rumors is exceedingly important—not only to protect people against negligence, cruelty, and unjustified damage to their reputations, but also to ensure the proper functioning of democracy itself.

Afterword, 2013: Bacon Is Shakespeare

This little book was completed in December 2008, about a month before I joined the Obama administration, first as a senior adviser to the director of the Office of Management and Budget, and then as the administrator of the Office of Information and Regulatory Affairs. The latter position is subject to the Senate confirmation process, and because of the nature of that process, I was able to see some of the dynamics discussed here at very close range. I will get to them in due course. But I want to begin with William Shakespeare, not with twenty-first-century politics.

Edwin Durning-Lawrence was a writer and a member of the UK Parliament who devoted much of his life to an obsessive, and slightly crazy, effort to demonstrate that Francis

Bacon wrote the works usually attributed to Shakespeare. Durning-Lawrence published his defining book, *Bacon Is Shakespeare*, in 1910.[89]

Bacon, a contemporary of Shakespeare, was an influential philosopher who also served as a member of Parliament. Durning-Lawrence greatly admired Bacon, but he didn't much like Shakespeare, whom he describes as an illiterate and, more specifically, as "the mean, drunken, ignorant, and absolutely unlettered, rustic of Stratford who never in his life wrote so much as his own name and in all probability was totally unable to read one single line of print."

In *Bacon Is Shakespeare*, Durning-Lawrence endeavored to show that all available evidence unambiguously supports the thesis of the book's title. A famous engraving of Shakespeare, he claims, actually provides clues that Shakespeare was not an author at all; Shakespeare's alleged signatures are forgeries. According to Durning-Lawrence, all proof of Shakespeare's authorship turns out to establish exactly the opposite.

In his closing chapters, Durning-Lawrence gets pretty wound up. Chapter 9 ends, "The hour has come when it is desirable and necessary to state with the utmost distinctness that BACON IS SHAKESPEARE." The conclusion of chapter 10: "It is not possible that any doubt can any longer be entertained respecting the manifest fact that BACON IS SHAKESPEARE." Chapter 11's final words, on two volumes by Bacon and Shakespeare, respectively: "These two title pages were prepared with consummate skill in order to reveal to the world, when the time was ripe, that BACON IS SHAKESPEARE."

Durning-Lawrence's appendix collects the names of famous people who appeared to agree with his thesis. Enlisting the rhetorical strategy now known as "social proof,"

Durning-Lawrence concludes, "The names that we have mentioned are amply sufficient to prove to the reader that he will be in excellent company when he himself realizes the truth that BACON IS SHAKESPEARE."

Despite his obsessiveness, Durning-Lawrence was an intelligent and accomplished person. His inadvertently hilarious book is an extreme case of a far more general (and much less hilarious) phenomenon through which people do not evaluate evidence on its merits, but instead enlist it opportunistically in support of their preordained conclusions. In the pages of this book, I focus on the phenomena of biased assimilation and confirmation bias. Durning-Lawrence was a gold medalist in biased assimilation and a world champion of confirmation bias.

Durning-Lawrence was quite colorful, but his is actually a minor contribution to a massive volume of writings on the authorship of Shakespeare's works.[90] That literature provides a series of fascinating studies in the transmission of rumors. In the Great Shakespeare Authorship Wars, all of the mechanisms discussed here have played an important role—not merely biased assimilation and confirmation bias, but also informational cascades, conformity cascades, and group polarization. Propagators of authorship-related rumors have been both persistent and ingenious. And there is an unmistakable similarity between the Shakespeare authorship wars and modern political arguments, in which people with entrenched points of view repeatedly assert, on the basis of those rumors that they accept, some version of BACON IS SHAKESPEARE.

When I served in government from 2009 to 2012, my principal role was to help oversee regulation (involving, for example, health, safety, and the environment), and among other things to reduce the risks of excessive or unjustified regulatory costs. On a number of occasions, the Obama administration declined to go forward with costly rules, on the ground that they would impose excessive burdens and promote undue uncertainty. Within the administration, we were acutely aware that when government imposes large costs on the private sector, it is not some faceless, inhuman abstraction called "business" that foots the bill. Workers and consumers might have to pay as well—and increased costs are especially unwelcome to those who do not have a lot of money. Nonetheless, many people on the left treated any decision to postpone regulations, or not to go forward with them, as confirmation of the following allegedly eternal truth: BUSINESS INTERESTS CONTROL GOVERNMENT. Baseless rumors, often involving what supposedly happened in secret meetings or suggesting some nefarious "cave" to powerful private interests, helped to shore up belief in that basic idea.

Bacon-Is-Shakespeare-ism has no particular ideology; it is hardly limited to those on the left. There are plenty on the right. A small example: in June 2013, the Obama administration announced that it would postpone until 2015 enforcement of Obamacare's so-called employer mandate, which will require employers with more than fifty employees either to provide health insurance or to face significant financial penalties. Emphasizing that the underlying reporting requirements are unusually complicated, the administration said that a one-year delay would allow the government to try to simplify those requirements while creating more flexibility for the private sector. The vast majority of large employers already provide health insurance, and so a one-year delay was unlikely to have significant adverse effects on workers.

To those who deplore the health-care law, however, the real lesson of the announcement is clear: OBAMACARE IS A DEBACLE. To the Obama administration's critics in Obama's second term, that was, and is, the real lesson of essentially every development in health-care reform. As with Durning-Lawrence, so with many of Obamacare's critics, whose conclusions are both motivated and preordained. For both the left and the right, it is child's play to identify many such conclusions, often consisting of, or backed by, rumors of one or another sort.

Since this book was published, I have frequently been asked how my experience in Washington changed my views about the transmission of rumors. I continue to think that the mechanisms described here capture the essentials, but on reflection, they underrate the *opportunistic or strategic use of rumors*—sometimes by interest groups, sometimes by political operatives of one or another sort, sometimes by politicians themselves. Such rumors often make their way into the news media. They can be widely noticed, especially by those with a keen political interest, and then a vicious cycle might begin, in which they seem to attain the status of established truth. Facts and figures can count as rumors, and in Washington, certain rumors, allegedly from a reputable source, attain the status of urban legends.

This is certainly true in my own area of government regulation. One alleged study found that in 2008, the total cost of regulation in the United States was $1.75 trillion, well over $10,000 per worker. Wow—but the study is full of mistakes and the numbers are essentially worthless.[91] I was asked to testify before Congress on numerous occasions, and on one of them, I tried to explain the worthlessness of that particular study, but I don't think I made much progress. On another occasion, I was asked to comment on a bit of research on regulatory burdens, obviously written by people with an agenda, that had the words "talking points" in big letters in the upper right-hand corner. Questioned about that research, I responded that in Washington, I had learned that any study with the words "talking points" on the first page was unlikely to be objective. (I confess that no one smiled or nodded, or even seemed to have any idea what I was talking about. In Washington, "talking points" are the coin of the realm.)

In a kind of destiny's joke, this very book was subject to the same dynamics that it discusses. My primary focus is of course on the transmission of rumors, and nothing here argues in favor of censorship (notwithstanding a brief and tentative discussion of libel law). But many people reported that the book's central goal is to restrict freedom of speech. One headline: "Obama's In House Communist Czar Cass Sunstein Wants to Censor the Right Wing Rumor Mongers." Another: "Cass Sunstein's Despicable Ideas on Regulating the Internet." Another: "Is a New Sedition Act on the Way? Czar Sunstein, Cowboy Hired by Obama to 'Corral' the Bloggers."

In one account, the book was described as advocating "a more insidious form of thought control a la 1984." While my Senate nomination was pending (not the best timing), a review in the *New York Post* stated that "Sunstein . . . who has been appointed to a shadowy post that will grant . . .

powers that are merely mind-boggling, explicitly supports using the courts to impose a 'chilling effect' on speech that might hurt someone's feelings. He thinks that the bloggers have been rampaging out of control and that new laws need to be written to corral them."[92] Another reviewer stated that this book "is a blueprint for online censorship as he wants to hold blogs and web hosting services accountable for the remarks of commenters on websites while altering libel laws to make it easier to sue for spreading 'rumors.'"[93] Yet another wrote, "In the best tradition of Stalin's commissars, Cass Sunstein had called for muzzling the extreme right wingers."[94]

Many presidential nominees are subject, of course, to close scrutiny, and legitimately so, and rumors about their actions and beliefs can go viral. Those who disseminate such rumors might well be outraged, frightened, or alarmed—and they may even be right. What I want to emphasize here is the role of opportunism and strategizing. Propagators may hope to attract dollars or eyeballs. They might seek to obtain fame, friendship, admiration, or respect. They might want to undermine someone whom they do not much like (perhaps the president). And when people accept false rumors that spread through processes of this sort, they may not be at all irrational or badly motivated. On the contrary, they learn from those whom they trust.

In a brilliant essay, the political scientist Russell Hardin urges that extremists suffer from a "crippled epistemology," in the sense that they know very few things, and what they know is wrong.[95] The essay is brilliant partly because it illuminates how all of us, whatever our views, learn about topics with which we lack personal familiarity. Those who accept false rumors may or may not be extremists, but they may well have little (relevant) information, and their views are supported by what little they know. Because they trust (or want to trust) those who convey false rumors, their views may become entrenched and essentially impervious to correction. In their view, BACON IS SHAKESPEARE. They may well process the information that they receive, whatever its content, in light of that central truth. All of us are capable of Bacon-Is-Shakespeare-ism, and when things go badly wrong in the political domain, it is often because of the kinds of polarization that separate people with firm, but opposing, views about who wrote *Hamlet* and *King Lear*.

But there is also good news, and it too reflects what I learned in Washington. Whatever their political affiliation, elected officials are almost always generous and courteous, and in private, they tend to be far more tentative and cautious than they are in public. Within the executive branch, we were not much moved by rumors, unless we had good reason to believe that they were true. Bizarre, fact-free claims—or wild distortions of beliefs and actions—might receive a lot of attention on the Internet or among genuine extremists, but public officials generally do not have trouble dismissing them for what they are. This is not at all to say that false rumors are never a problem. On the contrary, they can cause serious harm in both campaigns and actual governance. But the system of checks and balances, alongside the healthy skepticism of experienced officials, provides important safeguards.

Though Bacon was not Shakespeare, he said it well, at the opening of the *Novum Organum*: "They who have presumed to dogmatize on Nature, as on some well-investigated subject . . . have inflicted the greatest injury on philosophy and learning. For they have tended to stifle and interrupt inquiry exactly in proportion as they have prevailed in bringing others to their opinion."

Stratford's William Shakespeare said it better:

> . . . Ignorance is the curse of God,
> Knowledge the wing wherewith we fly to heaven.
>
> (*2 Henry VI*, 4.7)

Acknowledgments

I am grateful to many people who helped with both the original and the revised edition of this book. Many of the core ideas grew out of a paper prepared for a conference held at the University of Chicago Law School in November 2008; my thanks to Saul Levmore, my co-panelist, and Martha Nussbaum, the co-organizer of the conference, for valuable comments and suggestions. Nussbaum deserves special thanks for numerous and continuing discussions of this topic. Thanks too to Edward Glaeser for help in developing some of the ideas here and for joint work on this topic. My agent, Sarah Chalfant, initiated the process that transformed the paper into a book. My amazing editor on the original edition, Thomas LeBien, turned out to be a true collaborator on the project; the book is far better for his detailed thoughts and suggestions. Special thanks to Lauren Lepow for superb copyediting of the paperback edition. My wife, Samantha Power, was a great help throughout.

Notes

1. See Cass R. Sunstein and Adrian Vermeule, "Conspiracy Theories: Causes and Cures," *Journal of Political Philosophy* 17 (2008): 202–27, from which I borrow for this paragraph.

2. See Mark Lane, *Plausible Denial: Was the CIA Involved in the Assassination of JFK?* (New York: Thunder's Mouth Press, 1991) (arguing that it was); Alan Cantwell, *AIDS and the Doctors of Death: An Inquiry into the Origins of the AIDS Epidemic* (Los Angeles: Aries Rising Press, 1988) (suggesting AIDS was the product of a biowarfare program targeting gay people); Don Phillips, "Missile Theory Haunts TWA Investigation; Despite Lack of Evidence and Officials' Denials, Some Insist Friendly Fire Caused Crash," *Washington Post*, March 14, 1997, A3; the statements of Senator James Inhofe ("With all the hysteria, all the fear, all the phony science, could it be that manmade global warming is the greatest hoax ever perpetrated on the American people? I believe it is."), 149 *Cong. Rec.* S10022 (daily edition, July 28,

2003); David Mills, "Beware the Trilateral Commission! The Influential World Panel Conspiracy Theorists Love to Hate," *Washington Post*, April 25, 1992, H1 (describing various conspiracy theories about the commission); William F. Pepper, *An Act of State: The Execution of Martin Luther King* (New York: Verso Books, 2003) (arguing that the military, the CIA, and others within the government conspired to kill King); Kevin Diaz, "Findings Don't Slow Conspiracy Theories on Wellstone Crash," *Star Tribune* (Minneapolis), June 3, 2003, A1; Patty Reinert, "Apollo Shrugged: Hoax Theories about Moon Landings Persist," *Houston Chronicle*, November 17, 2002, A1.

3. See, e.g., James Fetzer, *The 9/11 Conspiracy* (Chicago: Catfeet Press, 2007), and Mathias Broeckers, *Conspiracies, Conspiracy Theories, and the Secrets of 9/11* (Joshua Tree, Calif.: Progressive Press, 2006). The latter book sold over 100,000 copies in Germany.

4. Cass R. Sunstein, *Why Groups Go to Extremes* (New York: Oxford University Press, 2009).

5. *Abrams v. United States*, 250 U.S. 616, 630 (1919) (Holmes, J., dissenting).

6. Gordon W. Allport and Leo Postman, *The Psychology of Rumor* (New York: Henry Holt, 1947), 503.

7. Leon Festinger, *A Theory of Cognitive Dissonance* (Evanston, Ill.: Row, Peterson, 1957).

8. Timur Kuran, *Private Truths, Public Lies* (Cambridge, Mass.: Harvard University Press, 1998); Marc Granovetter, "Threshold Models of Collective Behavior," *American Journal of Sociology* 83 (1978): 1420.

9. I draw here on David Hirshleifer, "The Blind Leading the Blind: Social Influence, Fads, and Informational Cascades," in *The New Economics of Human Behavior*, edited by Mariano Tommasi and Kathryn Ierulli (Cambridge: Cambridge University Press, 1995), 188, 193–95, and on the discussion in Cass R. Sunstein, *Why Societies Need Dissent* (Cambridge, Mass.: Harvard University Press, 2003), 55–73.

10. John F. Burnham, "Medical Practice à la Mode: How Medical Fashions Determine Medical Care," *New England Journal of Medicine* 317 (1987): 1220, 1201.

11. Hirshleifer, "Blind Leading the Blind," 204.

12. Sushil Bikhchandani et al., "Learning from the Behavior of Others: Conformity, Fads, and Informational Cascades," *Journal of Economic Perspectives* 12 (1998): 151, 167.

13. For many illustrations, see Terry Ann Knopf, *Rumors, Race, and Riots* (New Brunswick, N.J.: Transaction, 2006).

14. Matthew J. Salganik et al., "Experimental Study of Inequality and Unpredictability in an Artificial Cultural Market," *Science* 311 (2006): 854–56.

15. Ibid.

16. Matthew J. Salganik et al., "Leading the Herd Astray: An Experimental Study of Self-Fulfilling Prophecies in an Artificial Cultural Market," *Social Psychology Quarterly* 71 (2008): 338.

17. Fabio Lorenzi-Cioldi and Alain Clémence, "Group Processes and the Construction of Social Representations," in *Blackwell Handbook of Group Psychology: Group Processes*, edited by Michael A. Hogg and R. Scott Tindale (Oxford: Blackwell Publishing, 2001), 311, 315–17.

18. See the overview in Solomon Asch, "Opinions and Social Pressure," in *Readings about the Social Animal*, edited by Elliott Aronson (New York: W. H. Freeman, 1995), 13.

19. Solomon Asch, *Social Psychology* (Oxford: Oxford University Press, 1952), 453.

20. Asch, "Opinions and Social Pressure," 13.

21. Ibid., 16.

22. Ibid.

23. Micah Edelson et al., "Following the Crowd: Brain Substrates of Long-Term Memory Conformity," *Science* 333, no. 6038 (2011): 108–11.

24. Aronson, *Readings about the Social Animal*, 23–24.

25. Robert Baron and Norbert Kerr, *Group Process, Group Decision, Group Action* (Pacific Grove, Calif.: Brooks/Cole, 1992), 66.

26. Kuran, *Private Truths, Public Lies*.

27. Allport and Postman, *Psychology of Rumor*, 35.

28. Reid Hastie, David Schkade, and Cass R. Sunstein, "What Really Happened on Deliberation Day," *California Law Review* 95 (2007): 915–40.

29. Roger Brown, *Social Psychology*, 2nd ed. (New York: Free Press, 1986).

30. J.A.F. Stoner, "A Comparison of Individual and Group Decision Involving Risk" (unpublished master's thesis, Massachusetts Institute of Technology, 1961).

31. Lawrence Hong, "Risky Shift and Cautious Shift: Some Direct Evidence on the Culture Value Theory," *Social Psychology* 41 (1978): 342.

32. Ibid.

33. Serge Moscovici and Marisa Zavalloni, "The Group as a Polarizer of Attitudes," *Journal of Personality and Social Psychology* 12 (1969): 342.

34. Ibid.; Brown, *Social Psychology*, 210–12.

35. Hong, "Risky Shift and Cautious Shift."

36. John C. Turner et al., *Rediscovering the Social Group: A Self-Categorization Theory* (New York: Blackwell, 1987), 142–70.

37. Ibid., 153.

38. Ibid.

39. Paul Cromwell et al., "Group Effects on Decision-Making by Burglars," *Psychological Reports* 69 (1991): 579, 586.

40. Norris Johnson et al., "Crowd Behavior as 'Risky Shift': A Laboratory Experiment," *Sociometry* 40 (1977): 183.

41. Ibid., 186.

42. E. Allan Lind et al., "The Social Construction of Injustice: Fairness Judgments in Response to Own and Others' Unfair Treatment by Authorities," *Organizational Behavior and Human Decision Processes* 75 (1998): 1.

43. Robert Baron et al., "Social Corroboration and Opinion Extremity," *Journal of Experimental Social Psychology* 32 (1996): 537.

44. Mark Kelman et al., "Context-Dependence in Legal Decision Making," *Journal of Legal Studies* 25 (1996): 287–88.

45. Baron et al., "Social Corroboration and Opinion Extremity," 537.

46. Allport and Postman, *Psychology of Rumor*, 182.

47. Tolga Koker and Carlos L. Yordan, "Microfoundations of Terrorism: Exit, Sincere Voice, and Self-Subversion in Terrorist Networks" (unpublished manuscript 2008), available at http://papers.ssrn.com/sol3/papers.cfm?abstract_id=1286944.

48. Allport and Postman, *Psychology of Rumor*, 182.

49. Marc Sageman, *Leaderless Jihad* (Philadelphia: University of Pennsylvania Press, 2008).

50. Ibid., 116.

51. Ibid.

52. See Joseph Henrich et al., "Group Report: What Is the Role of Culture in Bounded Rationality?" in *Bounded Rationality: The Adaptive Toolbox*, edited by Gerd Gigerenzer and Reinhard Selten (Cambridge, Mass.: MIT Press, 2001), 353–54, for an entertaining outline in connection with food choice decisions.

53. Edward Glaeser, "Psychology and Paternalism," *University of Chicago Law Review* 73 (2006): 133.

54. John G. Bullock et al., "Partisan Bias in Factual Beliefs about Politics" (unpublished working paper, 2013), available at http://www.nber.org/papers/w19080.pdf.

55. In the context of rumors, this point is illuminatingly explored in the classic treatment by Allport and Postman, *Psychology of Rumor*, 105–15.

56. See, e.g., Lee Ross et al., "Perseverance in Self-Perception and Social Perception: Biased Attributional Processes in the Debriefing Paradigm," *Journal of Personality and Social Psychology* 32 (1975): 880, and Dan M. Kahan et al., "Biased Assimilation, Polarization, and Cultural Credibility: An Experimental Study of Nanotechnology Risk Perceptions" (unpublished manuscript, 2008), available at http://papers.ssrn.com/sol3/papers.cfm?abstract_id=1090044.

57. Brendan Nyhan and Jason Reifler, "When Corrections Fail: The Persistence of Political Misperceptions" (unpublished manuscript, 2008) (available from authors).

58. See Ross et al., "Perseverance in Self-Perception and Social Perception."

59. Charles S. Taber et al., "The Motivated Processing of Political Arguments" (unpublished manuscript, 2008), available at http://papers.ssrn.com/sol3/papers.cfm?abstract_id=1274028.

60. Nyhan and Reifler, "When Corrections Fail."

61. Ibid., 13.

62. Ibid., 12.

63. Ibid., 14.

64. Brendan Nyhan et al., "The Hazards of Correcting Myths about Health Care Reform," *Medical Care* 51 (2013): 127–32.

65. Carl I. Hovland and Walter Weiss, "The Influence of Source Credibility on Communication Effectiveness," *Public Opinion Quarterly* 15 (1951–52): 635–50.

66. Festinger, *Theory of Cognitive Dissonance*.

67. Kahan et al., "Biased Assimilation, Polarization, and Cultural Credibility."

68. Cass R. Sunstein, *Laws of Fear* (New York: Cambridge University Press, 2006).

69. Edward L. Glaeser and Cass R. Sunstein, "Why Does Balanced News Produce Unbalanced Views?" (working paper, 2013), available at http://papers.ssrn.com/sol3/papers.cfm?abstract_id=2230996.

70. Prashant Bordia and Nicholas DeFonzo, "Problem Solving in Social Interactions on the Internet: Rumor as Social Cognition," *Social Psychology Quarterly* 67 (2004): 33; see generally Nicholas DeFonzo and Prashant Bordia, *Rumor Psychology* (Washington, D.C.: American Psychological Association, 2006).

71. Tamotsu Shibutani, *Improvised News: A Sociological Study of Rumor* (Indianapolis: Bobbs-Merrill, 1966), 46.

72. Knopf, *Rumors, Race, and Riots*.

73. Chip Heath et al., "Emotional Selection in Memes: The Case of Urban Legends," *Journal of Personality and Social Psychology* 81 (2001): 1028.

74. Ibid., 1032.

75. Ibid., 1038–39.

76. *Cox Broadcasting Corp. v. Cohn*, 420 U.S. 469 (1975).

77. Ibid.

78. Daniel Solove, *The Future of Reputation: Gossip, Rumor, and Privacy on the Internet* (New York: Oxford University Press, 2008).

79. I am grateful to Larry Lessig for pressing this point.

80. For a catalog, see http://www.chillingeffects.org/.

81. *New York Times Co. v. Sullivan*, 376 U.S. 254 (1964).

82. Ibid.

83. *Gertz v. Robert Welch, Inc.*, 418 U.S. 323 (1974).

84. Ibid.

85. *Time, Inc. v. Hill*, 385 U.S. 374 (1967).

86. Cf. *Hustler Magazine v. Falwell*, 485 U.S. 46 (1985).

87. For a valuable and provocative discussion, see Eugene Volokh, "Freedom of Speech, Information Privacy, and the Troubling Im-

plications of the Right to Stop People from Speaking about You," *Stanford Law Review* 52 (2000): 1049.

88. *Zeran v. America Online, Inc.*, 129 F.3d 327 (4th Cir. 1997).

89. See Edwin Durning-Lawrence, *Bacon Is Shakespeare* (London: Gay and Hancock, 1910).

90. A superb overview is James Shapiro, *Who Wrote Shakespeare?* (New York: Simon & Schuster, 2010).

91. Robb Mandelbaum, "Questions on a Study of the Cost of Federal Regulation," *New York Times*, April 10, 2013, available at http://boss.blogs.nytimes.com/2013/04/10/questions-on-a-study -of-the-cost-of-federal-regulation/.

92. Ed Lasky, "Cass Sunstein's Despicable Ideas on Regulating the Internet" (2009), available at http://www.americanthinker.com /blog/2009/07/cass_sunsteins_despicable_idea.html.

93. Ibid.

94. William McCullough, "Obama's In House Communist Czar Cass Sunstein Wants to Censor the Right Wing Rumor Mongers," (2009), available at http://www.commentsonnationalamnesia .com/2009/11/24/obamas-in-house-communist-czar-cass-sunstein -wants-to-censor-the-right-wing-rumor-mongers/.

95. Russell Hardin, "The Crippled Epistemology of Extremism," in *Political Extremism and Rationality*, edited by Albert Breton et al. (Cambridge: Cambridge University Press, 2002), 3, 16.